FAT-BACK & MOLASSES

A Collection
of Favourite Old Recipes
from Newfoundland & Labrador

Edited by Ivan F. Jesperson
Graphics by Lorie M. Jesperson
(when 12 years of age)

Published by:
Jesperson Publishing

P.O. Box 2188, 100 Water Street, St. John's, Newfoundland, A1C 6E6

Reprinted 2002, 2004, 2006, 2008

Preface to Fourth Edition of Fat-Back & Molasses — January, 1989

This Fourth Edition of *Fat-Back & Molasses* is dedicated to the people of Newfoundland and Labrador wherever they may live on planet earth. Since the First Edition in 1974, *Fat-Back & Molasses* has found its way into more than 100,000 homes of Newfoundlanders on the island and around the world.

Fat-Back & Mollasses is more than a cookbook. Certainly its recipes bring an array of foods into combinations that tantalize the critical gourmet and everyday family appetites alike—but the book's success has also been enhanced by the beautiful culture it reflects. It mirrors an image of a people whose pristine character has been carved from four centuries of living on the "Rock". The delightful names of their recipes and the colour of their humour reveal a people whose imagination is still very much alive and in communion with nature and the joy of life.

Fat-Back & Molasses is an authentic part of Newfoundland and Labrador. If you have not visited Canada's newest province, then read this book first for the pleasure of meeting your most easterly neighbours, then enjoy some of its recipes. It is the next best thing to visiting Newfoundland and Labrador and sharing in the experience of one of the shining jewels in the fabric of Canadian culture.

Ivan F. Jesperson

Preface to First Edition of Fat-Back & Molasses - July 1974

This book would not have been possible, but for three things. The first is the love that I have received from the people themselves of Newfoundland and Labrador. During the past six years residence in this province as a clergyman, many doors of all denominations have been opened to me. In the homes the white table cloth has always been placed with respect and the table set with friendliness. The meals prepared have been garnished with experience and un-equaled in flavour. Out of this hospitable background has grown my first inspiration to capture on paper how the Newfoundland and Labrador women have triumphed in the kitchen.

My second debt is primarily to the United Church Women from many of the smaller communities of Newfoundland and Labrador. Through their co-operation and welcome support most of the recipes found in this book have come. I am also indebted to a small mimeographed booklet entitled "The Labrador Cookbook" for a few of the enclosed recipes. This latter publi-cation was edited by some community spirited people to raise money to send some of their children on an exchange visit to other provinces. Their failure to put their names on the publica-tion speaks even more highly of their dedication.

My third indebtedness is to my daughter, Lorie, who drew the seasonal sketches of outport Newfoundland when she was twelve years old. Each of them were familiar scenes on Fogo Island that made a deep imprint in her mind as the seasons rolled by. Fortunately for me, she was able to sketch on paper the rich pageantry of the outport life.

I. F. Jesperson

ALPHABETICAL INDEX OF RECIPES

Butterscotch Fingers, 104; Butter Balls, 146; Caramel Sauce, 138; Chocolate Crackers, 127; Chocolate Cream, 145; Christmas Balls, 144; Cherry Oat Crumble, 81; Christmas Dominoes, 139; Date Cocoanut Macaroons, 146; Date & Nut Bars, 108; Fat Back & Lassy Toutons, 108, Fine Puff Pastry, 86; Frosty Fruit Pie, 84; Golf Balls, 114; Graham Wafer Pie, 84; Honey Tarts, 107; Ice Cream Delights, 139; Jam Jams, 147; Lassie Jam Tarts, 80; Lemon Sponge, 85; Lemon Sponge Pie, 85, Light Patty, 131; Martha Washington Pie, 122; Molasses Tart, 135; Pineapple Surprises, 135; Raisin Pie Fillng, 86; Rhubarb - Marshmallow Dessert, 135; Soft Custard, 80; Snow Balls, 121, Snowball Dessert, 82; Spanish Cream Dessert, 102; Yum Yums, 12.

BARS, SQUARES — Apricot Bars, 142; Apricot Filling, 142; Blueberry Squares, 133; Brownies, 141; Butter Scotch Squares, 125; Caramel Squares, 134; Cherry Chews, 143; Chocolate Cocoanut Squares, 141; Coctail Squares, 139; Cut Glass Squares, 123; Date Squares, 134; Ice Cream Squares, 138; Jelly Squares, 123; Lemon Squares, 104, 116, 140; Maids of Honour, 143; Malted Milk Squares, 140, 143; Marshmallow Squares, 141, 142; Orange Squares, 137; Partridgeberry Squares, 106; Peach Squares, 137; Peach-Rice Loaf Supreme, 132; Strawberry Squares, 140.

PUDDINGS - Figged Duff, 77; Figgy Duff with molasses Coady, 78; Bread Pudding, 69, 76; Boiled Apple Pudding, 76; Blueberry Pudding, 81; Boiled Pudding, 108, Christmas Steamed, 75; Lassy Coady Dumplings, 78, Molasses Steam Pudding, 146; Pork Bang Belly, 77; Baked Rice, 79; Southern Rice, 79; Partridgeberry Cottage, 79; Mom's Apple, 80; Hard Times Pudding, 75; Dark Suet Pudding, 72; Steam Pudding, 69; Molasses Pudding, 69; Quick Apple Pudding, 70; Pudding sauce, 70; Steam Molasses Pudding, 70.

CAKES — Banana, 91; Blueberry, 90, 133; Boiled, 51; Birthday, 101; Cocoa, 100; Cake Made in a Hurry, 92; Coffee, 132; 1,2,3,4 Cake, 124; Corn Syrup Frosting, 125; Dark, 91; Fat Pork, 87; Home Made Icing, 125; Mace, 110; Miracle, 92; Molasses, 96; Mystery Icing, 109; Dark Cake, 88; Date, 90 Overseas, 101; Peach, 102; Pineapple Upside down, 105; Potato Pork, 87; Raisin-Apple Coffe Cake, 101; Sponge, 94; Sultan, 74; Susie's Icing, 109; Tomato Soup Cake, 97; Walnut Cake, 91.

FRUIT CAKES — Dark Christmas, 110; Old Fashioned Christmas, 111, 112, 113; Mrs. Smallwood's Fruit Cake, 100; Fruit Cake, 99; Grandma's Favourite Dark Cake, 99; Boiled Fruit Cake, 97; Dark Fruit, 94, 95, 96; Light Fruit Cake, 97; Pineapple Fruit Cake, 107, Rich Wedding Cake, 113.

COOKIES - Black & White, 127; Blueberry, 114; Caramel Nut, 129; Chocolate Cream, 129, Centenial, 131; Cry Babies, 101; Drop, 130; Ice Cream Cookies, 131; Marble Cookles, 125;, Marshmallow, 118; Mince Meat, 116; Old Time, 117; Parowax, 116; Peanut Butter, 118; Pudding Cookies, 127; Raisin Drop, 128; Raisin & Nut, 118; Ruby Cookles, 130; Rice Krispie, 132;, Saucepan Cookies, 127.

AFTERS - Brown Sugar Candy, 138; Bull's Eyes, 105; American Ice Cream, 70; Lassie Pop, 147; Molasses Taffy, 137.

WINES, BRANDY, BEERS — Apricot Brandy, 149; Dandelion Wine, 148; Old Time Barm, 156; Partridgeberry Punch, 149, Rhubarb Brandy, 149; Rice Wine, 148; Spruce Beer, 126, 156; Uncle Allen's Blueberry Wine, 150.

GRACES FOR THE TABLE

Submitted by Mr. K. Porter, aged 90 (died 1975)

1. Grant us thy blessings
   on these thy gifts,
   Through Jesus Christ
   our Lord. Amen.

2. For these and all other mercies
   May the Lord's name be praised
   Now and forever,
   through Jesus Christ our Lord. Amen.

3. Give us this day our daily bread,
   Let us by thy hand be lead,
   Keep our hearts from wrong today,
   In thy holy name we pray. Amen.

4. For the food upon our table,
   For the birds outside our door,
   We thank the Heavenly Father
   For these things and many more. Amen.

5. As we meet around this table
   Our hearts unite in praise
   to thee our Heavenly Father
   Who blesses all our days. Amen.

6. Be near to us in breaking bread
   and do not then depart.
   Saviour, abide with us and
   spread thy table in our heart. Amen

7. Dear Father, take us by the hand
   and lead us through this day.
   Bless this food and teach us
   thy loving ways to pray. Amen.

8. From thy hand cometh every good,
   We thank thee for our daily food.
   Now, with it Lord thy blessing give
   And to thy glory may we live. Amen.

FISH & BREWIS

"The following recipe is a typical Newfoundland dish which everyone learns to love, even the English Methodist Parsons." Dinner for two:

Break up and soak in cold water overnight two cakes of hard bread. If all the water is absorbed by morning add a little more to keep it from burning. Place to boil and add 1/2 tsp. salt. When water boils up all through it, strain and chop into small pieces with a fork.

Boil about 1 lb. of well watered salt fish for 20 minutes. Strain. Flake it into small pieces and remove bones.

Add to the hard bread mixture and drip pork fat & scrunchions over it.

Take a piece of fat back pork (about 1/2 lb) and cut in thin slices and fry until crisp and brown. Break up pork in small bits with fork and knife. Drip over fish & brewis on a dinner plate.

Mrs. Florence Wilkinson - Moores, Topsail

FISHERMAN'S BREWIS

Skin and bone fresh fish. Put in boiling salted water and cook until tender. Soak hard bread overnight. Put the soaked bread into cold water; bring slowly to the boil and cook only until tender, 5 - 10 minutes. Fry out small pieces of fat pork. Add the cooked fish, then the cooked brewis. Toss lightly and heat thoroughly.

This recipe famous over all Newfoundiland.

FISHERMAN'S BREWIS

4 cakes hard bread   fat back pork   salt   salt fish

Soak 4 cakes of hard bread overnight in plenty of cold water. Drain next morning and add more water. Add 1 tsp. salt and bring to a boil for five minutes. Drain very dry. Boil salt fish which has been watered for several hours. Drain fish then add fish to strained bread and chop both well together. Fry out small pieces of fat back pork to cover heapings of Fisherman's Brewis served on plate.

Violet M. Gullford, Hant's Harbour

THE STORY OF FISH AND BREWIS

In the land where cod is king it is to be expected that many of our dishes make use of this delicious and versatile fish. Here in Newfoundland if you mean salmon, trout or halibut, you say so, but if you just say fish, you mean cod. Perhaps the most popular dish is Fish and Brewis, pronounced "broos'.

The New Englanders make fish and brewis too, but few people inland ever heard of it. In fact, one mainlander on first hearing of it, thought it had some connection with a still for making home brew. On the other hand a story is told of a clergyman newly come from England whose hostess asked him before he retired his first night if he would like fish and brewis for breakfast. Wishing neither to offend nor to be reckless, he replied cautiously that he would like fish, "but only one brew, please."

Newfoundland families in all income brackets and in all geographical locations serve fish and brewis with varying frequency, especially for Sunday morning breakfast. Sometimes the brewis is served with bacon or ham instead of fish. The fish, of course, is the salt fish and the brewis is made from the hard bread which can be bought in the grocery stores here. As in all such dishes an exact recipe is hard to find, each cook having her own way of doing the cooking which gives a slightly different flavour to the finished product.

FISHERMAN'S BREWIS

Salt fish as required   Hard bread as required   Fat pork as required

To Prepare Brewis: Split cakes of hard bread; allow 1 cake per person. Place in a large saucepan well covered with water. Soak overnight. The next day, using same water bring to near boil. (do not boil). Drain immediately. Keep hot. To prepare fish, soak salt fish overnight, changing water once. Boil for 20 minutes until fish is flaky. Drain and remove skin and bones from fish. Combine fish and hard bread together. Serve with scrunchions (small cubes of fat pork fried to golden brown).

Annie Mugford, Clarkes Beach, Nfld

A LONG DISTANCE CALL HOME TO NEWFOUNDLAND

My daughter, Peg, was born and raised in Newfoundland and no doubt saw plenty of fat pork used in our home. She married and moved to Toronto to live. One day she decided to have company in for a "fish and brewis' dinner. She went to the Newfoundland Market and purchased the items needed. Everything went well until she came to preparing the fat pork. She did not know what to do with it. So she hurriedly made a long distance call home to me asking "Mom, how much fat will I put on the fry pan to fry out the fat pork?"

Mrs. Lillian Babstock, St. John's, Nfld.

FRIED COD HEADS

Obtain 4 medium size cod heads. More for a large family. After they have been sculped - ((to sculp heads: with sharp knife cut head down through to the eyes; grip back of head firmly and pull)) - prepare to cook as follows:

Cut heads in two, skin and remove lips. Wash well and dry. Dip both sides of head in flour, sprinkle with salt and pepper to taste. Fry in fat until golden brown on both sides. Serve with potatoes and green peas, or any vegetable preferred.

Mrs. Lloyd G. Hann, Wesleyville, B. B. Bay

COD FISH CHOWDER

1 lb. fresh frozen cod fish	dash of sugar & pepper	2 tbsp. butter	2 tsp. salt
2 cups cooked potatoes, diced	1 cp. evaporated milk	1/3 diced onion	3 cups water

Combine butter, onion, potatoes, water, salt, sugar and pepper. Boil gently for about 15 minutes. Once cooked, add fish and simmer gently until cooked, about 10 minutes. Add milk and heat slowly, but do not boil.

Recipe from "Labrador Cook Book" Happy Valley & Goose Bay, Labrador

BAKED CODFISH

1 small codfish	pepper	1 onion	salt	salt pork

sufficient bread for dressing

Fry out sufficient salt pork to make fat enough to cook the fish in. Prepare dressing enough to stuff fish. Then place dressing in fish and sew it up to keep dressing in.

Place the prepared fish in roaster, where fat has already been thrown. Cut up onion and put in with a little water. Sprinkle with salt and pepper. Bake in moderate over for about 1 1/2 hours. Serve with potatoes.

Recipe from Barbara Bixby, Stag Harbour

CODFISH CUSTARD

1 1/2 tspns. cornstarch   1 1/2 cups milk   2 eggs beaten   1/4 cup melted butter
1/2 tspn. salt   2 cups flaked codfish

Dissolve cornstarch in milk and add the beaten eggs, melted butter and salt. Stir in flaked codfish and pour into greased 1 quart casserole. Bake in 350 F. oven for 45 minutes, or until the custard is firm.

Recipe from Eva Combden of Barr'd Islands

FISH BAKED IN CUSTARD

1 lb. fresh fillets   1 cup milk   1 tbsp. margarine   2 eggs   salt & pepper to taste

Cook fillets in the milk until tender. Add salt & pepper to taste. Remove from stove & add margarine. Beat eggs slightly & add hot milk to them. Place fish in a casserole. Pour mixture over it & place casserole in a pan of hot water. Bake at 350F for 45 min. or until custard is firm.

Recipe from Fogo Island U.C.W.

BAKED CODFISH

Small fish is best. Remove head, tail, fins, & sound bone from fish. Wash well and dry with paper towel. Stuff as for chicken (beaten egg may be added to dressing). Fry fat, pour over fish. After fish is brown on one side, turn over and brown other side. Bake for approx 60 min. at about 450 F. If preferred, onions & scrunchions may be added.   *United Church Women - Fogo Island*

BAKED STUFFED FISH

Choose a whole fish, about 3 or 4 pounds; remove head, wash & wipe dry. Sprinkle inside with salt & fill with a well seasoned stuffing. Secure the opening with skewers or sew it and lay the fish back up on a fish sheet (tin foil would be the modern solution).

Make diagonal gashes in the skin of the back and insert strips of salt pork or bacon (preferably pork). Place a little pork in the pan, dredge with flour and bake in a hot oven (400 F) about 1 hour, basting often with the fat in the pan.

Can be served often with white sauce and baked potato or any vegetable.

United Church Women - Mrs. Hedley Butt, St. Georges.

FISH PIE

1 can codfish or salmon	1/4 cup butter	2 onions	3 tbsp. flour
1/4 cup warm milk	1 1/2 cups potato water		

Cook onions in butter then remove pan from stove & mix in flour using fork to stir. Add water slowly, stirring all the time. Add fish & return to stove to thicken. Mash potatoes well while hot with 1/4 cup warm milk & butter. Add 1 egg unbeaten & mash well. Spread potato mixture over the fish & bake in hot oven until golden brown. Serve with green peas or carrots.

"I believe this recipe is very old as it was given to my mother back in the early 1900's. It has been passed down through the family for many years. It's a good recipe and a very delicious meal."

Mrs. Meta Beazley, Garden Cove U. C. W.

FISH LOAF

2 cups fresh codfish (boiled)	1 1/2 cups bread crumbs	onion & parsley chopped fine
2 eggs	1/2 tsp. savoury	pepper & salt to taste

Combine mixture & bake 1 hour in moderate oven.

Mrs. Joan Brown of Joe Batt's Arm.

DEEP FRIED FISH

Batter: 1 cup milk   1 egg   1/2 cup flour   few grains salt

Cut fish in squares & salt. Dip each piece in batter until completely covered, then place in boiling fat until golden brown.   *Thelma Freake of Joe Batt's Arm.*

FISHERMAN'S FRESH FISH STEW

4 slices fatback	5 lb. fresh codfish	1 med.onion or chives
potatoes	pepper	water

Place fatback in a pot; let fry out well. Clean fish thoroughly, wash and remove skin; cut in squares about 2 inches. Add fish to fat and then add sliced onions or chives. Slice potatoes 1/4 inch thick and cover fish with potato slices; season. Add 3/4 cup boiling water (more if needed). Cook slowly until potatoes and fish are tender (about 1/2 hour). Serves 6.

Mrs. Ella Herridge, Little Bay East & Mrs. Heber Fifield, Wesleyville

SCRAD

"Catch a fresh fish. Bring it in and split him, wash him, and sprinkle a little salt and put him out for 2 hours in the sun. Then shake off the salt and bring him up and put him in the oven in a flat pan. Bake for 1/2 hour. Remove from oven and he's ready to eat."   *Mrs. Stan Pope, Fogo, N.D. Bay.*

JANUARY shows the woodsman bringing his annual supply of firewood from the woods. One of my most treasured Newfoundland experiences was accompanying several men from Joe Batt's Arm on one of their winter treks into the forest. The dry crisp snow squeeked under the runners of the sled while the harness bells jingled to the pace of the horses. It was like stepping into a Christmas card. Then when it was time to eat; plastic pails and weathered canvas bags revealed the nourishing pleasures which would make any outdoor gourmet gallop. The prize of them all was the famous Newfoundland 'rounder' roasted over the open fire. Its succulent flavours were enough to make the new day welcome when the men had to go into the woods again.

BARBECUED FISH

1 1/2 lb. fillets	1/4 cup table vinegar	2 tblspns. chopped onion
1 tblspn. worcestershire sauce	1 tblspn. shortening	2 tblspn. brown sugar
3/4 cup tomato ketchup	1/2 tspn. salt.	

Heat oven to 375 F. Place fish in shallow baking dish (greased). Brown onion lightly in shortening in small saucepan. Add other ingredients, simmer for 5 minutes and pour over fish. Bake for 30 minutes, or until fish is tender.

Above recipe from Mrs. N. Holmes of Seldom Come By, Fogo Island.

FISH SOUFFLE

3 1/2 tblspns. butter	2 cups milk	3 1/2 tblspns. flour	2/3 tspns. salt
1/8 tspn. paprika	2 cups cooked fish	1/3 cup bread crumbs	2 eggs

Melt butter, add flour and when smooth, stir in milk. Cook until thickened. Add seasoning & crumbs. Cool. Add flaked fish to sauce & mix well. Stir in egg yolks, and stiffly beaten whites. Put in greased baking dish & bake in moderately hot oven until firm.

Above recipe from Grace Roberts of Joe Batt's Arm

FISH PIE

Line a greased baking dish with mashed potato. Fill the dish with minced cooked codfish (salt or fresh). Cover generously with drawn butter & onions. Add another layer of mashed potatoes. Bake 30 minutes in a slow oven.

Jubilee Guild of Newfoundland & Labrador

FISH CASSEROLE

2 cups cooked cod or haddock   4 hard cooked eggs   1 1/2 cups white sauce
4 med. sized cooked potatoes   2 tblspns. margarine   1/2 cup day-old bread crumbs

1. Bone & flake fish & place 1/2 of it in bottom of a margarine coated casserole dish.
2. Slice eggs and lay over fish.
3. Cover with 1/2 of the white sauce
4. Cover with 1/2 of the potatoes, sliced.
5. Repeat these layers again.
6. Melt margarine & add crumbs. Sprinkle over top of casserole.
7. Bake in moderately hot oven, 400 F. about 20 minutes. (Serves 6-8)

Mrs. William H. Anthony, Burnt Point, Seldom Come By.

BAKED COD TONGUES

24 cod tongues   2 tblspns. salt   1 cup milk   1 cup biscuit or bread crumbs

Wipe cod tongues with damp cloth. Soak in milk in which salt is dissolved for about 10 minutes. Drain and roll in crumbs. Place on greased sheet or dish and bake in 450 F. oven for about 10 minutes. Serve with lemon slices.

Recipe from Ellen Keats of Barr'd Islands

HOW TO FRESHEN DRIED SALT FISH: Shred fish, wash it several times in fresh cold water. Cover with fresh cold water and bring to a boil. Pour off water and repeat the operation depending on the amount of salt in the fish. Do not cut dried, salt fish with a steel knife as the fish will have a "steely" taste.

"Canadian Fish Recipes" Dept of Fisheries of Canada

TUNA FISH UPSIDE DOWN PIE

1 small can tuna fish   1 can mushroom soup

Put fish in strainer and let hot water run over it to remove oil. Let drain. For the crust mix with hands 1 cup flour, a little salt, 1 tsp. baking powder and 3 or 4 tbsp. of lard to make a dough. Then butter pie tin, cover plate with chunks of fish, and then cover with mushroom soup and spread biscuit dough over top and bake 20 or 30 minutes. Turn out on platter and add a little parsley for decoration.

"Labrador Cook Book" Happy Valley, Goose Bay, Labrador

BAKED STUFFED FISH

4 tablespoons butter	2 cups soft bread crumbs	2 teaspoons minced onions
1/4 teaspoon salt	stuffing	dash of pepper

Use whole fish cleaned and dressed. Rub inside of fish with salt. Stuff loosely as dressing will expand during cooking. Sew up opening in fish with needle and thread. Place fish on greased racks in shallow uncovered pan.

Bake at 375 F. allowing 10 minutes per pound. If fish is dry - while cooking baste with the juice from the bottom of the pan or lay strips of bacon or salt pork across the fish or brush with French dressing.

Recipe from U.C.W. - Fogo Island.

BAKED FISH LOAF

15 1/2 oz. tin salmon, tuna	3/4 cup milk	1 egg, beaten	chopped parsley
or 2 cups leftover cooked fish	1/8 tsp. pepper	1 to 2 tsp. lemon juice	1/2 tsp. salt
1 cup stale bread crumbs			

Flake fish and combine with other ingredients. Mix well & pack into a greased loaf pan. Bake at 350 F. until firm & browned (30 to 40 Minutes). Turn from mould and serve hot with or without white sauce.

"Labrador Cookbook."

BANQUET BAKED FISH

1 whole fish or large section	1 onion finely diced	3 tbsp. butter	**3 tbsp. flour** seasoned with
3 cups small bread cubes	1 tsp. dried leaf savory	1/2 tsp. salt	1/2 tsp. savory
1/4 tsp. sage	sprinkle of pepper	1/2 cup water	1/4 tsp. sage
1/4 lb. mild cheese, grated or finely diced			1/4 tsp. salt
			sprinkle of pepper

Saute onion in butter. Add to bread cubes with seasoning, water and 1/2 of the cheese. If too dry add more water.. Pack stuffing firmly inside and in front of fish. Dredge all over with seasoned flour. Bake with 3/4 cup of hot water in bottom of pan until browned and tender, about 50 minutes at 350 F, basting frequently.

While fish bakes cream 4 tbsp. butter with 1/4 cup flour, add juice of 1 lemon or 3 tbsp. juice (bottled), 3 tbsp. sugar, and 1 1/2 cups of water. Cook over low heat, stirring until thickened. Add to gravy in pan with remaining cheese. Baste fish again with thickened gravy.

"This recipe for Banquet Baked Fish, now included in the manuscript for "The Man Pleasers' Cook Book", was created one summer in Cupids, Miriam Dawe's birthplace, during the early nineteen thirties. We jigged cod in the harbour with our dear old neighbour, Chris Bishop, who always knew just where we should lower our jigger to haul up a fresh, round beauty. A few years later the recipe was a prize winner in The American Weekly Magazine, Boston. Now, in the seventies, we can no longer find a whole cod in any market, only an occasional haddock to substitute. The wonderful big Newfoundland fish is just a tantalizing memory. Even whole, dried, salt fish have disappeared."

From Margaret Hunt Stanhope, daughter of Miriam Dawe Hunt.

NEWFOUNDLAND SAYINGS: "Long may your big jib draw." - A good wish for the future; in other words, "May there always be wind for your sail."

Submitted by United Church Women of Swift Current

FRIED COD TONGUES

Carefully wash fresh cod tongues and dry in a paper towel. Allow 7 or 8 per person. Put 1 1/2 cups flour, 1 teaspoon salt, 1/2 teaspoon pepper together in a plastic bag. Put tongues in and shake them until evenly floured. Cut up 1/2 pound salt pork and fry until golden brown. Remove pork cubes and fry tongues until golden brown on both sides.

Serve with mashed potatoes and green peas. *Recipe from Margaret Freake of Joe Batt's Arm.*

BAKED COD TONGUES - Wipe the cod tongues with a damp cloth, place in salted milk (1/2 cup milk to 1 tblspn. salt). Roll each in breadcrumbs, place on a greased baking sheet and cook 10 minutes in a very hot oven. Serve with Tartar Sauce. *Fish Favourites' - by the Jubilee Guilds of Nfld. & Lab.*

COD SOUND PIE

2 lb. salt cod sounds	2 cakes hard bread	1 tsp. spice	1/2 cup molasses
1/2 lb. salt pork	1/2 tsp. cloves	1 tsp. cinnamon	1 cup raisins

Soak Sounds in cold water for 24 hours. Drain sounds, and cover with fresh cold water. Cook until tender. Chop in small pieces. Previously soak hard bread for 12 hours in cold water, break in small pieces after draining, and then add to tender sounds. Cut salt pork in tiny squares, mix in raisins, molasses and spices and pour mixture over sounds and hard bread. Place all in pan and bake for two hours in moderate oven (350 F).

"This recipe came from Western Head, Notre Dame Bay, and may originally have come from our great-great grandparents who came from England. It was always served for Christmas Eve Supper. The Sounds were brought from Labrador where our fathers fished in the summer months. The Sounds were salted down in wooden tubs. Butter was bought then in 22 and 10 pound wooden tubs. Today, where Sounds are available, the fifth generation of our family still has "Cod Sound Pie" on Christmas Eve and it really is a delicacy." Mrs. Stella Boyd, Summerford

COD SOUNDS

2 lb. salt cod sounds   4 strips salt pork   shallots or onions

Put about 2 lb. of salt cod sounds in water & let stand overnight, then drain off water. Put in a saucepan and cook for about 10 minutes. Drain. Fry pork, cut up shallots or onions, then cut sounds in small pieces and fry altogether. Add a little water if necessary.

"This recipe was used some 80 years ago, and often, for a Sunday evening meal with home made bread and butter. It was enough for the family and very tasty and delicious. Today, mashed potatoes, french fries, whole potatoes with green peas could be served with this dish."

Mrs. Winnifred Green, Hants Harbour

FISH CHOWDER

1/4 lb. salt pork   1/3 cup cold water   2 cups hot milk   1/3 cup flour
2 cups hot water   sprinkle of pepper & 1 tsp. salt   2 or 3 med. onions peeled & sliced 1/8"
2 lb. boneless fish, fresh or frozen, bite size   4 med.potatoes, peeled & sliced 1/3" thick

Cube salt pork in about 1/2" size. Fry in heavy kettle or Dutch Oven until crisp & golden. Remove pork scraps & reserve. Saute onions in pork fat until tender & transparent but not browned. Add potatoes, hot water, salt, and pepper. Boil 5 minutes.

Add fish & simmer until potatoes are tender & fish flakes easily, 5 to 10 minutes. Mix flour & cold water to a smooth paste, add to chowder & stir gently to keep from burning without breaking up the potatoes & fish. When thickened add hot milk & sprinkle pork scraps over top. Serve with hot crusty rolls or hot biscuits and butter. Even more delicious the next day, reheated.

Above recipe from "The Man Pleasers" Cook Book Manuscript by Margaret H. Stanhope of Crescent Road, Lunenberg, Mass. and is used with her permission.

FISH CHOWDER

2 lb. fresh fish	1 med. onion	2 cups milk	salt & pepper
2 cups boiling water	2 tbsp. butter	potatoes, sliced	carrot, sliced

Melt butter, slice onion, cook until onion is transparent or until tender. Add salt & pepper. Cut fish into small pieces. Add fish & cook about 15 minutes longer. Add milk & simmer. Do not boil.

United Church Women - Swift Current

FISH CHOWDER

3 slices salt pork,diced	1/8 tsp. pepper	2 tbsp. butter	1/3 cup sliced onions
1/2 cup water	soda biscuits	1 lb. fish fillets	1/2 tsp. salt
3 cups milk	1 1/2 cups sliced potatoes		

Fry salt pork until golden brown; add onions & cook slowly until tender. Add potatoes, salt, pepper & water. Cover and cook for 10 minutes. Add fish & cook for 15 minutes, adding more water if necessary. Add milk & butter and heat. (Do not boil) Serve with crushed soda biscuits over the top.

U. C. W. - Mrs. Ella Herridge - Little Bay East

FISH CHOWDER

1 lb. fresh frozen cod fish	2 tbsp. butter	1/3 cup diced onion	2 tsp. salt
2 cups cooked potato diced	3 cups water	dash of sugar & pepper	1 cup evaporated milk

Combine butter, onion, potato, water, salt, sugar & pepper. Boil gently for about 15 minutes. Once cooked, add fish, simmer gently until cooked - about 10 minutes. Add milk & heat slowly, but do not boil.

United Church Women - Fogo Island

FISH CHOWDER

1/4 lb. fat salt pork, sliced
3 cups boiling water

6 small potatoes
salt and pepper to taste

2 onions, chopped fine   1 pint milk
2 cups diced uncooked fish

Fry salt pork in a deep pot. When crisp remove pieces of pork and put fish, potatoes and onions in pot. Cover with boiling water and simmer one-half hour, or until potato is tender. Add the milk and cook five minutes longer. Season to taste with salt & pepper. (Serves 5)

This recipe has been traditionally used by busy fishermen at work on the sea and comes from the ' College of Fisheries' of St. John's, Nfld.

CODFISH VEGETABLE CASSEROLE

1/4 cup chopped onion
1/4 tspn. paprika

1 tbsp. butter
2 cups flaked codfish (fresh)

2 cups white sauce
1 cup corn kernels

1/2 tsp. pepper
1 cup cooked carrot
or mixed vetetables.

Fry onion in butter until tender. Combine with other ingredients and season with salt to taste. Pour into greased casserole and cover with pastry dough. Bake in 425 F. for 30 minutes.

This recipe comes from Eva Combden of Barr' d Island.

SOUSED HERRING OR MACKEREL

Clean fresh herring or mackerel. Place in shallow baking dish. Make a mixture of vinegar, enough to cover fish, and add sugar, pepper and salt to taste and about a tablespoon of mixed pickling spice. Bake in oven until tender. Serve when cold with boiled or baked potatoes.

Grace Roberts, Joe Batt's Arm

DEEP FRIED CAPLIN

1 dozen caplin	1/2 cup flour	1/2 cup milk	1 egg
1/2 tsp. salt	l tsp. oil or butter	1/2 tsp. baking powder	

Clean caplin, removing heads and tails, then wash and dry them on a paper towel. Beat eggs, add oil, flour, salt, baking powder and milk. Beat well. Dip fish in batter. Deep fry in hot oil or fat until golden brown (3 to 5 minutes). *Native Cookery & Edible Wild Plants of Newfoundland & Labrador*

BAKED STUFFED SQUID

6 squid	1/2 tsp. salt	2 cups bread crumbs	1 onion chopped
2 tsp. melted butter	1 tsp. poultry seasoning		

Clean squid by removing tentacles and skin; then wash and sprinkle with salt. Make dressing and stuff squid. Sew up or skewer. Wrap in aluminum foil, putting strips of fat back pork in each squid. Bake at 350 F. for 3/4 hour. *Native Cookery & Edible Wild Plants of Newfoundland & Labrador*

CHEESE - CELERY SAUCE for SALMON

1 can (10 oz.) condensed cream of celery soup	2 tbsp. milk	1 can salmon (1 1/2 lb)	cooked rice
	1 cup shredded old cheddar cheese		1/2 tsp. worcestershire
1 cup mixed vegetables.			

In top of double boiler place soup & 2 tbsp milk. Blend until smooth & heat thoroughly. Add liquid & cheese and sauce. Flake salmon and add to sauce & mix in vegetables. Cover & heat thoroughly. Border a heated platter with rice & centre with salmon mixture.

"This recipe has been used as far back as early 1900 and comes from the Canadian Home Journal."
Flora D. Luther, Sunnyside, Newfoundland.

FEBRUARY in Newfoundland is reserved for the hearty men who wave aside the fierce sting of blowing snow and icy wind, for their hearts glow warm at the thought of turrs, puffins and tickle-aces. For hours, days and sometimes weeks they shelter by the spraying shore and unload their barking muzzleloaders into the clouds of sea birds that tantalize their appetite.

A TOAST: "Here's to the women - God created them beautiful and foolish.
Beautiful so the men would love them; foolish so they would love the men."

Submitted by Mrs. Florence Wilkinson-Moores

LAKE TROUT WITH DRESSING

2 lbs. lake trout fillets	1 tsp. mixed poultry seasoning	2 tsp. salt
1/2 cup minced onion	4 cups dry bread crumbs	4 tbsp. butter or fat

Wipe fish fillets with damp cloth. Sprinkle with one teaspoon salt and place in a greased baking dish. Mix dry bread crumbs, poultry seasoning, and one teaspoon salt. Saute onions in melted butter or fat and add to bread crumb mixture. Arrange stuffing over fish and put a cover over the dish.

Bake at 400 F., allowing 10 minutes per inch thickness of fish. Remove cover after 10 minutes to brown dressing. (Serves 6)

Recipe from Memorial University of Newfoundland Extension Service

SAVOURY CODFISH

Place the contents of 1 can of codfish in a buttered casserole. Cover with white sauce as follows:

Melt 2 tablespoons butter then add 2 tbsp. flour, seasoned with pepper & 1 tsp. salt. Stir in 1 cup milk and cook until thick.

Sprinkle over above with dressing made with:

1 cup bread crumbs	1 tablespoon butter	1 tablespoon savoury

Crumble all together and place bacon strips on top. Bake 20 - 30 minutes.

FISHERMAN'S FRESH FISH STEW

4 slices fat back   potatoes   5 lbs. fresh fish   water   1 med. onion or chives.

Place fat back in pan & fry out well. Clean fish thoroughly, wash and remove skin. Cut in squares about 2 inches. Add fish to fat and then add sliced onions or chives. Slice potatoes 1/4" thick and cover fish with the potato slices. Season. Cook slowly until potatoes and fish are tender. (1/2 hour) Serves six.

Mrs. Ella Herridge, Little Bay East & Mrs. Heber Fifield, Wesleyville

COD AU GRATIN

4 cups (2 lbs) cooked cod fillets   3 tbsp. flour   2 cups milk   1/2 tsp. salt
1 cup grated sharp cheddar cheese   3 tbsp. butter or fat   1/8 tsp. white pepper

Flake fish. Make white sauce with fat, flour, salt, pepper and milk. Stir until thickened. Arrange fish in bottom of dish or individual servings. Cover fish with cream sauce & top with grated cheese. Place casseroles in shallow pan of water and bake at 350 F. for 30 minutes.

United Church Women, St. John's, Nfld.

FISH PUDDING

1 med. wt. fish   1/4 cup milk   1 or 2 onions   6 soda crackers
1 tin tomato soup

Cook fish in salted sater, strain and remove bones. Place fish in bowl with soda crackers broken in crumbs. Stir in other ingredients and mix well. Place in greased baking dish and bake 1/2 hour. Cover dish while baking.

Mrs. Claude Ford, Fogo, Nfld

BAKED TURBOT

Split turbot, clean, wash & drain thoroughly. Cut into squares & place in a greased baking dish, skin side down. Sprinkle with salt & pepper. Bake in a moderate oven until brown, draining fat off the fish from dish as it collects.
Jubilee Guild of Newfoundland & Labrador

BAKED CODFISH PIE

Line a 1 1/2 quart baking dish with mashed potatoes well covering the bottom. Nearly fill the dish with boiled salt-cod which has been minced or finely shredded. Add about 1 cup drawn butter sauce made with a little chopped onions. Spread a thick layer of mashed potatoes over the fish and bake at 350 F. for 30 to 40 minutes.
Above recipe from United Church Women of Fogo Island

COD FISH CAKES

2 onions chopped	3 cooked parsnips	1 egg well beaten	1/4 tsp. pepper
2 cups salt codfish, boned, cooked		1/2 cup bread crumbs	6 cooked potatoes

Cook onions in a very small amount of water. Mash together fish, potatoes, parsnips. Add onions, water in which they were cooked. Season. Add beaten egg and combine well. Form in cakes, roll in bread crumbs and fry in rendered pork fat.

"This recipe is used in Newfoundland very often for the supper meal and is often made from left-overs of salt cod & potatoes."
Mrs. R. Hudson, St. Geroges

ROAST CAPLIN: Put 6 or 7 dozen fresh caplin in 1 1/2 gallons water. Sprinkle with 1 cup of coarse salt or 1 1/2 cups fine salt. Soak overnight. Then spread out doors in sunshine for 2 or 3 days. Roast in hot oven about 15 minutes. Good with hot home made bread and partridgeberry jam.
United Church Women Fogo Island.

IT ISN'T APRIL IN ST. JOHN'S WITHOUT FLIPPER PIE

Flipper pie means 'seal flipper pie' and is made from the fore-paws from seal flippers. In the Spring when the first sealing ship comes down from the ice of Labrador or the Gulf with its hold packed with seal- skins, it will also carry some barrels of flippers for sale in St. John's. So eager are the customers that the first flippers sell for $12 to $18 a dozen. Each cleaned flipper would weigh from one-half to one pound. Nearly all the Men's Clubs in St. John's serve a flipper supper sometime in April and tickets are sold out long ahead of time. The meat is tender and tasty, but you have to be born in Newfoundland to really appreciate it. Few mainlanders acquire a great liking for it, but it isn't April in St. John's without at least one flipper pie. *Mrs. Harvey Lambert, Twillingate, N.D. Bay*

FLIPPER PIE

Clean flippers well, making sure to cut off all fat. Some people parboil the flippers about 20 minutes. Dredge with flour. Add seasoning and put in pan with fat back pork, onion and bacon. When nearly cooked, about 2 hours, vegetables may be added and a rich biscuit type topping put on. The meat should be tasty and tender when cooked. Serve with lemon wedges.
Recipe from "Labrador Cook Book", Happy Valley & Goose Bay, Labrador

NEWFOUNDLAND FLIPPER PIE

4 seal flippers	1 qt. water	1 tsp. soda	1 tsp. salt
1/2 cup pork fat diced	2 onions, chopped	1 tsp. flour	1 cup cold water
1 tsp. worcestershire sauce			

Soak flippers in water and soda for 1/2 hour. Trim off all excess fat. Dip flippers in seasoned flour and pan fry in pork fat to brown.
Add chopped onions. Make a gravy of flour, water and worcestershire sauce. Pour over flippers. Cover and bake in moderate oven (350 F.) until tender, 2 to 3 hours. Cover with pastry and bake at 400 F. for last 1/2 hour.
Native Cookery & Edible Wild Plants of Newfoundland & Labrador

BAKED FLIPPER

2 flippers	1 turnip	6 potatoes	salt & pepper
3 slices salt pork	2 carrots	2 onions	1 parsnip

Soak flippers for 1/2 hour in cold water to which has been added 1 tbsp. baking soda. Remove fat from flippers, wash and cut in serving pieces.

Fry out the pork and remove the scrunchions. Brown flippers in this fat. Then add water and sear until partly tender. Add onion and vegetables, except the potatoes. Season and add more water. Cook about 1/2 hour, then add potatoes. Cook another 15 minutes. Cover with your favourite pastry and bake at 425 F. for 20 minutes.   *United Church Women - Swift Current, Plac. Bay.*

FLIPPER PIE

Do not parboil the flippers as this makes a disagreeable odour and permeates the meat. Take the flippers and soak in cold water with 1 tablespoon soda for 1/2 hour. The soda makes the fat snow white. Remove the fat. Render out fat pork, dip flippers lightly in salted flour and fry until brown in the pork fat. Take from frying pan when brown and put in a covered roasting pan in a medium oven. Add onions if desired. Make gravy, pour over flippers and allow to cook until tender. They may then be put in pastry as a pie or served as they are, garnish with parsley and lemon.

Recipe from Mrs. Tom Best

'SCOFF' -   A meal, especially one hastily served up aboard a vessel.
Now it has come to mean a ' boiled dinner' or party late at night.

E. R. Hann, Wesleyville, B. B., Nfld..

LOBSTER STUFFED EGGS

6 hard cooked eggs
2 tbsp. mayonnaise

1 cup cooked lobster
salt & pepper

1 tspn. prepared mustard
paprika

Cut eggs in half and remove the yolks to a bowl. Mash yolks well & stir in lobster, mustard, mayonnaise and seasonings. Spoon into the egg whites and sprinkle top with paprika. Chill before serving.
Memorial University of Newfoundland and Labrador

LOBSTER FRITTERS

1 cup chopped lobster
1 1/4 cups flour

2 eggs   1/2 cup milk
2 teaspoons baking powder

salt & pepper to taste

Heat deep fat until a cube of bread browns in sixty seconds. While fat is heating, beat eggs until light . Add milk and flour sifted with baking powder, salt & pepper, then fold in chopped lobster. Drop by small spoonfuls into fat, fry until golden brown. Drain on brown paper in warm oven. Serve with quick lemon sauce.

To make sauce, combine 1 cup lemon or orange or pineapple marmalade, 1 tspn. grated lemon peel, 1 tblspn. vinegar and 1/2 cup boiling water. Place in covered jar & shake until well mixed.
Memorial University of Newfoundland Extension Service

DRAWN BUTTER

1/2 cup butter   2 1/2 tspns. flour   2 small onions   1 1/2 cups hot water

Melt butter in small saucepan; add onions & cook for a few minutes over low heat. Add the flour & blend thoroughly. Add hot water & cook until thickened, stirring constantly. Salt & Pepper to taste.
Margaret Freake - Joe Batt's Arm.

JIGGS DINNER

"The following recipe is designed either for a large family or for a public occasion:"

Take a large piece of salt meat and soak in cold water over night. Next, place fresh water in the pot and boil salt meat on the stove with a small amount of salt pork for 45 minutes or longer. While that is boiling, prepare your vegetables. Cut your turnip in small pieces, peel carrots, potatoes and prepare cabbage. Add vegetables to the boiling pot, beginning with turnips, then carrots, cabbage and lastly the potatoes, allowing 15 minutes between each vegetable. Cook until the potatoes are done.

If cooking for your own family, a cup of peas placed in a cloth and tied with a string may be hung in the pot to cook with your salt meat dinner before the vegetables are placed in. They should be soaked in cold water first though. *"This makes a good family dinner." - Mrs. Norah Leyte, Fogo.*

POTATO PANCAKES

6 medium potatoes	1/8 tsp. pepper	1 tbsp. grated onion
5 tbsp. flour	1/4 tsp. baking powder	1 tbsp. minced parsley
1 1/2 tsp. salt	2 eggs well beaten	cooking oil or fat

Combine flour, salt, pepper and baking powder. Set aside. Wash, pare and finely grate potatoes to make about 3 cups. Drain off surplus liquid. Combine flour mixture with eggs, onion and parsley. Add grated potatoes and beat thoroughly with a spoon. Spoon about 2 tbsp. batter into hot, well oiled heavy frying pan, leaving about one inch between pancakes. Cook over medium heat until golden brown and crisp on one side. Turn over and brown other side. Drain on paper towel. Serve as an accompaniment to sausages, pork chops, or fried ham.

To serve with apple sauce, syrup or sprinkle, omit pepper & onion.

United Church Women - Swift Current, Nfld.

NEWFOUNDLAND STEW

1 to 1 1/2 lb. salt meat	1 small head cabbage	1 medium turnip
1 onion	4 medium carrots	6 medium potatoes

Cut up salt meat and cover with hot water to remove salt. Let soak for about 15 minutes. Drain off water. Add 6 or 7 cups of cold water to meat in boiler and cook for 1 hour.

Pare and cut up vegetables and add to meat. Cook until vegetables are tender. The amount of vegetables added may depend on the number of dishes to be served. Above recipe serves six.

United Church Women - Fogo Island

ONE DISH MEAL

Put layer of sliced raw potatoes in bottom of greased casserole. Cover with a layer of onions then a layer of hamburger meat. Mix one tin of tomato soup with 1/2 tin of water. Season each layer with salt and pepper to taste. Bake for 1 hour. Makes a delicious meal.

Mrs.. Manuel Reid - Joe Batt's Arm

KEDGEREE

1 cup raw rice	2 hard cooked eggs	pepper to taste	1 tsp. chopped parsley
2 cups cooked fish	1/4 cup melted butter	1/2 tsp. salt	

Cook rice in boiling salted water until tender. Drain. Remove bones and skin and flake fish. Add to rice. Chop egg whites in small pieces. Mix with fish and rice. Melt butter in the top of double boiler. Add the fish mixture. Season with pepper and a small amount of salt if salt fish is not used. Heat thoroughly & serve garnished with chopped egg yolks. Use as little water as possible when cooking vegetables.

United Church Women - Fogo Island

FAT BACK PORK STEW

1/2 lb. pork	dash pepper & salt	1 medium turnip	1/2 tsp. salt
12 sliced potatoes	6 medium sized carrots	8 sliced onions	2 tablespoons catsup

Fry pork with onions until brown. After adding carrots and turnip, simmer for 15 - 20 minutes. Add potatoes and season with pepper and salt. Blend in catsup and boiling water, When partly cooked, cover with paste. To make the paste, use the following:

2 cups flour	pinch salt	3 tsp. baking powder	3/4 cup cold water.	2 tbsp. butter

Sift flour with baking powder and salt. After adding butter, mix with fork, Add water to make a soft dough; toss dough on floured board and roll out 3/4 inch thick. Place over stew. Cook 15 minutes or until done.

"Fat Back Pork Stew" is a Newfoundland recipe. It was often made by my grandmother, who, if living, would be over 100 years old."

Mrs. George B. Winsor, Cupids, Nfld.

MOOSE STEW

3 lbs. moose meat (cut up)	salt & pepper to taste	2 parsnips	1 small turnip
1/4 lb. salt pork	1 onion	6 cups water	2 carrots
10 potatoes			

Fry pork for 5 minutes. Add moose and brown in hot fat. Add water, salt and pepper. Let simmer. Add chopped onion after 1 hour of cooking. Cook for 1 hour, then cut up and add carrots, parsnip, turnip and potatoes. Cook for another 20 minutes. Make dumplings if you desire.

Jessie Hooper, Churchill Falls, Labrador.

MARCH is the month when the landsmen go out on the ice in search of seals. Sometimes the ice comes to shore and they walk from their homes to the frozen fields. Other times they must turn to their oars and heave to until their bow crunches the floating pan. Sealing is not "slaughter" in Newfoundland, but men in search of food and fur. Sealing is dangerous, hard work, where mistakes end with disaster; but like many other occupations sealing carries with it both the perils of disaster and the promise of glory. Every boy who goes out on the hunt returns a man. But all the promises of sealing are not for the spirit, for the Newfoundland sealer responds just as heartily to the rich aroma of baked flipper as he does to the large crowds greeting his ship returning to port.

LOB SCOUCE

1 lb. salt meat cubed	1 cup each of diced carrots,	1 parsnip, diced	2 tbsp. rice
1 med. onion diced	turnips and potatoes	1 cup chopped cabbage	

Soak meat overnight to remove the salt. Drain. Add 6 or 7 cups of fresh cold water, and cook for one hour. Then add the vegetables and rice. Cook until vegetables are tender. (Spareribs may be used instead of salt meat)

"Lob Scouce is a very thick soup or stew of vegetables and salt meat. A native of Liverpool, England, to this day is often called a "Lob-Saucer", so this is probably where this recipe originated. It has been used in Newfoundland for at least seventy years ."

Neta Ivany, Sunnyside and Miss Alice Lacey, Wesleyville

A NEWFOUNDLAND SAYING

"He's deaf as a haddock and she's foolish as a caplin."

Neta Ivany, Sunnyside, T. B., Nfld.

RABBIT STEW

2 rabbits	1/2 cup chopped celery	1 cup chopped onion	3 tsp. flour
fat pork	2 cups water	1 cup diced turnip	1 1/2 tsp salt
1/2 cup diced potato	3 carrots		

Cut up rabbit after cleaning. Dredge with flour and brown in pork fat. Then add vegetables and cook for 20 minutes. Thicken gravy. This may be served with dumpling or a pastry baked over it.

Native cookery & Edible Wild Plants of Newfoundland & Labrador

LABRADOR RABBIT STEW

1 - 3 lb. rabbit	1 tbsp. salt	1 cup uncooked carrot cubes	1/4 cup flour
1/2 cup cold water	1 large onion,diced	6 cups boiling water	dash of pepper
1 stalk celery,chopped		1 cup uncooked potato cubes	

Wash & cut up rabbit. Place in heavy kettle with onion, celery, salt and pepper. Add boiling water. Cover tightly and simmer for 2 hours. Add vegetables and continue simmering till vegetables are tender. Mix flour and water to paste, then thicken stew with this mixture. Serves 6

Recipe from"Labrador Cook Book"

BEEF and VEGETABLE STEW

2 lb. stewing meat,cubed	2 onions, sliced	1 tsp. Worcestershire sauce	3 tbsp. fat
1 1/2 cups quartered carrots	2 tsp. salt	6 stalks celery, 1" lengths	
4 large potatoes,quartered	1 cup peas	Pepper to taste	

3 cups hot water or 1 cup hot water & 2 cups tomato juice

Brown onions in fat. Roll cubed meat in seasoned flour and brown. Cover with hot water and tomato juice and simmer until meat is tender, about 1 1/2 hr. Add raw vegetables and cook until tender, about 30 minutes. Add cooked vegetables. Season to taste. If desired, thicken gravy with 2 tbsp. flour mixed with 1/2 cup cold water.

Recipe from Labrador Cook Book Happy Valley & Goose Bay, Labrador

MY BREAD STUFFING

3 cups bread crumbs	1 tsp. savory	1 egg	1/2 cup flour
1 onion cut very fine	1/2 tsp. salt	1/2 cup fat-back cut very fine	

Mix all together and stuff bird.

Mrs. E.A. Babstock, Corner Brook West, Nfld-

CHICKEN LIVER BREWIS

Soak at least 2 cakes of hard bread in water for at least five, hours or until soft. Add salt. Simmer, but do not boil. Fry liver with pepper and salt and onion. When fried, mix it in with brewis. Serve with pork grease and onions or Lemon butter sauce.

Recipe from Happy Valley, Goose Bay, Labrador

LABRADOR DINNER

Cook 2 lb. salt beef, cabbage, turnip, carrots, potatoes together. When meat and vegetables are cooked, add dough boys.

DOUGH BOYS

Blend 2 1/2 cups flour, 4 1/2 tsp. baking powder and 1 tsp. salt. Stir in water until mixture is moistened. Shape mixture into small balls and drop into liquid with the meat and vegetables. Cover pan tightly and cook for 15 minutes. Do not lift cover during cooking.

"Labrador Cook Book"

ONION PUDDING

1 cup flour	2 tbsp. butter	2 tsp. baking powder
1/3 cup milk	1/4 tsp. salt	1 med. onion grated fine

Rub butter into flour, baking powder and salt. Add grated onion and milk to make a soft dough. Place in small greased bowl (earthenware), cover top with wax papper and place in saucepan of boiling water. Keep boiling for half hour or more. Try centre of pudding with steel knitting needle for doneness.

"This recipe was used by the fishing vessels in spring when potatoes were scarce. It was also eaten with vegetables on the dinner plate. Good too." Mrs. Florence Wilkinson Moores, Topsail.

MY POTATO CAKES

Wash small potatoes, put in boiler and boil. When cooked, peel. Mash very fine. When mashed, mix with milk and butter. Take 2 eggs and beat yolks and mix with potatoes. Beat whites and spread on top. Put in oven, bake. A very fine dish with roasted caplin.

(A way to use up small potatoes)

Mrs. E.A. Babstock, Corner Brook

PORK PATTIES

2 lb. fresh pork	1 tsp. salt	2 tbsp. chopped onions	1/4 tsp. pepper
2 eggs well beaten	1 cup bread crumbs	1 tbsp. pork fat	

Wipe meat with damp cloth. Chop into very fine pieces. Mix with bread cubes, salt, onions, pepper, & eggs and form into patties. Melt fat. Fry patties on both sides over hot fire until well done, about 15 minutes.

"This recipe was given to me by my aunt and has been made and enjoyed by all."

Mrs. Joan Vincent - Newtown

OLD FASHIONED BAKED BEANS

2 lb. dried beans	1 med. onion sliced	1/4 cup tomato catsup	1 tsp. mustard
1/4 cup brown sugar	3/4 lb. salt pork sliced	1/16 tsp. pepper	1/2 cup molasses

Wash beans and add enough water to come two inches above beans. Boil until tender. Put in deep casserole mixed with other ingredients and bake until crisp and brown. Serve piping hot.

"This recipe was often used in the Lumbering Cabins."

Claris Vey, Hillview

CORNED BEEF

| 2 1/2 lb. salt beef | 6 med. sized potatoes | 1 small head cabbage |
| 1 lb. turnip | 1 lb. split peas | 1 lb. carrots. |

Soak salt meat in cold water over night. Before putting on to cook, cover with fresh water. Cook for 2 hours. Drain off stock and save for vegetables. Cover with boiling water & cook for 2 hours more. In stock drained from meat add cabbage, carrots, turnip one hour before serving. Add potatoes 1/2 hour before serving. (Serves 6)

This recipe often used by busy Longliner Crews and comes from the College of Fisheries, St. John's, Newfoundland.

PEAS PUDDING

Soak peas in pudding bag with salt meat over night. Cook same amount of time as meat. When mashing pudding add 1/4 lb. butter, tablespoon pepper and salt to taste. (Serves 6)

Recipe from College of Fisheries, St. John' s. Used often by fishermen.

SAUSAGES BAKED IN POTATOES

Wash and pare potatoes of uniform size. Make hole with apple corer in each. Push in sausage. Place potatoes in baking dish and bake in hot oven until soft. Baste every ten minutes with drippings.

Above recipe from Mrs. Maud Freake of Joe Batt's Arm.

BEEF OR VEAL STEWED WITH APPLES: Rub a stewpan with butter; cut the meat in thin slices, and put in with pepper, salt, & apple sliced fine. A little onion may be added. Cover it tight & stew till tender.

United Church Women - Fogo

SEVEN LAYER DINNER

Into a greased casserole dish place the following:
- 1 to 2 inches of thin sliced raw potatoes
- a layer of thinly sliced onion
- a layer of thinly sliced raw carrot

Then sprinkle 1/4 cup of uncooked rice over layers. Add 1 tin of green peas and liquid. Add one lb. of sausages. Pour 1 tin tomato soup (diluted) over all and bake in a moderate oven.

Thelma Freake - Joe Batt's Arm

CHICKEN FRIED RICE WITH SPARE RIBS

Fry one cup minced chicken (no bones) with one small onion and salt to taste. When tender, add 2 cups cooked rice, continue frying for 5 minutes over low heat. Bake two lbs. fresh spareribs with onions, salt & pepper. When spareribs are well done remove from pan and put on large platter. Garnish with chilli sauce or catsup. Serve with chicken fried rice.

Cynthia Coish - Stag Harbour

BARBECUED SPARERIBS

Boil spareribs for 10 minutes to remove fat.

Sauce:

1/2 cup brown sugar	2 onions	1/2 green pepper	1/2 cup vinegar
1 tsp. garlic sauce	1/2 tsp soya sauce	1 cup catsup	1 cup tomato paste

Mix together and simmer for 1/2 hour. If it is too thick, add water. Throw sauce over spareribs and bake at 350 F. for 2 hours.

Mrs. Cyril Martin, St. Vincent's, St Mary's Bay

BRUMSWICK STEW

2 squirrels	2 cups lima beans	6 potatoes	2 tsp. sugar
4 cups sliced tomatoes	2 slices lemon	1 tbsp. salt	6 ears corn
1 tsp. pepper	1/4 lb. butter	1 minced onion	1/2 lb. salt pork
flour			

Cut squirrel in pieces as for fricassee. Add salt to 4 quarts water & bring to boil. Add onions, beans, corn, pork, potatoes, pepper and squirrel pieces. Cover tightly and simmer 2 hours. Add sugar and tomatos and simmer 1 hour more. Ten minutes before removing stew from stove, add butter cut in pieces and rolled in flour. Boil up adding salt and pepper if needed. Pour in to dish and garnish with lemon.

"Labrador Cook Book" Happy Valley & Goose Bay, Labrador

SQUIRREL CAKES

3 squirrels	1 tbsp. catsup	2 tbsp. bread cubes
1/2 cup washed potatoes	1 onion, finely chopped	

Parboil squirrels in salt water for about 15 minutes, then remove all good meat. Grind bits of meat and blend with the bread crumbs, onion, catsup and washed potatoes. Mix well. Shape into small flat cakes and saute in hot bacon fat until well browned.

"Labrador Cook Book" Happy Valley & Goose Bay, Labrador

"My mother (who died last year at the age of 92 years) told me that when one of her girl friends was getting married over seventy years ago, she was asked to say the blessing. She started to say the grace 'For what we are to receive, O Lord, make us truly thankful.' But she said, "For what I am to receive," and all at the table burst into laughter."

Mrs. Mae Moulton, Burin Bay Arm

BRAWN

| meat from pigs | 4 nutmegs | head of cow or ox feet | salt & pepper |
| stock | other spices to taste | | |

Saw pig's head in 2 parts. Place in salt & water for 24 hours. Wash well, put to boil with sufficient cold water to cover completely. Skim and keep stock clear.

Saw in 2 or 3 parts 4 ox or cow feet (that is, the part from knee to joint above foot). Thoroughly wash and clean. Let almost come to a boil. Pour off this water & put down to boil with sufficient water to cover. Boil till almost jellied.

Remove bones. Mince meat from this and head. Strain stock from head and feet. Then combine strained stock & meat, add salt & pepper to taste, also 4 whole nutmegs grated and simmer for 1/2 hour. Pour into moulds.

M. M. Hollett, Burin, Newfoundland.

BARBECUE BEEF BALLS

| 1 cup soft bread crumbs | 1 tsp. salt | green pepper | 1/2 cup milk |
| 1 tsp. pepper | 1 lb. ground beef | 1 egg | |

Mix together, form into small balls and place in casserole. Then add 1 1/2 tsp. Worchester sauce, 1/2 cup water, 1/2 cup catsup, 1/4 cup vinegar, 3 tbsp. sugar, 1/2 onion chopped. Bake 1 hour at 350 F.

United Church Women - Swift Current

MACARONI CASSEROLE

Sauce:

| 1 can mushrooms | 1 pk. hamburger meat | 1 can tomatoes |
| 1 onion | 1 can Catelli meat sauce | |

Fry meat and onion. Drain off fat. Add the other ingredients and simmer for 1 hour. Boil 2 cups of macaroni. Pour sauce over macaroni mixing thoroughly. Bake at 350 F. for 1 hour.

Mrs. Cyril Martin, St. Vincent's, St. Mary's Bay

DUMPLING

1 lb. flour	1/2 lb. currants	2 tsp. baking soda (level)	1 lb. chopped suet
1 1/2 cups sugar	1/2 lb. raisins	2 tbsp. marmalade	2 tbsp. syrup
2 level tsp. each of cinnamon, ginger & mixed spice			

Mix all ingredients with enough milk so that mixture is rather dry and not too moist. Wet cloth in boiling water, then flour cloth. Put in mixture, tie cloth allowing for swelling. Bring water to boil. Place plate in bottom of pot. Put in dumpling and boil for 4 hours. Keep covering with boiling water.

Mrs. Eli Foote, Burin, Nfld.

MOM' S FRENCH FRY

		Thickening:
4 lb. potatoes	3 oz. diced salt pork	1/2 cup cold water
1/2 tsp. salt	1 onion any size	1/2 cup flour

First peel & slice potatoes or cut them small. Put them in a pot & cover with water. Add salt & bring to a boil. Meantime fry pork , add onion and cook until brown. Then add it to the potatoes. Continue cooking 1/2 hour or until potatoes are cooked. Make a thickening with the flour and cold water. Add to potatoes and cook for 5 minutes longer.

"The history of this French Fry must be known all over Nfld. But it sure is a favourite at our house when eight of us brothers and sisters raced home from school n the middle of the day and Mom would serve it piping hot with delicious homemade molasses bread and tea. One of my treasured memories."

Mrs. Norma Vey, Hillview, Newfoundland

NEWFOUNDLAND SAYING: "Did 1 ever get a roasting:" - Meaning, abuse or ridicule.

U. C. W. Swift Current, Nfld.

Mending Nets

APRIL is the month of preparation for the Newfoundland fisherman. He has his winter supply of wood standing on end in his garden. His fresh supply of birds and seals are bottled. Now he must prepare his fishing gear for the 'run' which surely will come in late May or early June. Climb into the loft of any fisherman's "store" and you will find him knitting new nets or mending old. Truly, this is the time when yarns are told, for treasured stories of the past help pass away the time. The crackling fire in a 45 gallon drum and the smack of 'baccy' only add to the rhythm of garnished yarns spun from the masters of story telling, the Newfoundland fisherman.

44

PANFRIED PARTRIDGE

2 partridge	3 tbsp. soft margarine	dash of pepper & celery salt	2 tbsp. flour
2 tbsp. hot water	1/2 tsp. salt	1 cup cream (18%)	

Remove feathers, head and entrails from partridge. Cut in half lengthwise. Combine flour, salt, pepper and celery salt. Dredge each portion thoroughly. Measure margarine into heavy frying pan, sear, then cook over lower heat until game is tender. Add mixture of hot water and cream during cooking. Lift partridge halves to heated platter. Pour over gravy. Serve 2 or 3.

"Labrador Cook Book" Happy Valley & Goose Bay, Labrador

ROAST PARTRIDGE

Pick and draw the same as chicken. Wipe inside and out with damp cloth rather than washing. Tuck the wings back and fasten the legs up to the sides of the body with a small skewer so that when the bird is on its back the legs stand up and not down towards the rump as it would with a chicken. Lard lightly and oven bake in moderate temperature, hot first, then slower for about 1 hour.

Serve on squares of toast. The partridge may be stuffed with dressing or a peeled cored apple placed inside. Serve with gravy and cranberry jelly.

"Labrador Cook Book" Happy Valley & Goose Bay, Labrador

PARTRIDGE SOUP

1 lb. salt beef	1 turnip	1 onion	tomato if desired
1 or 2 partridge	1 or 2 carrots	1/4 or 1/2 cup rice	

Fill pot almost full with hot water and add cut up salt beef and whole partridge. Let cook for 1 to 2 hours, or until cooked. Then add carrot, turnip and cut into small pieces. When almost cooked, add onion & rice. Boil till cooked.

"Labrador Cook Book"

SPLIT PEA SOUP

1 lb. salt meat or pork	2 quarts water	1 1/2 cups diced turnips
2 cups split peas	1 cup diced carrots	1/2 cup chopped onion

Cut salt meat in small pieces, soak for 10 minutes in warm water, then squeeze meat from water. Place in pot with the two quarts of water and peas. Let boil for 1/2 hour. Add all ingredients; carrots, turnip, onion and cook for 1 hour then serve.

Recipe from United Church Women - Fogo Island.

DUMPLINGS FOR ABOVE

2 cups flour	1 1/2 tsp. baking powder	1 tblspn. butter

Put all ingredients in a bowl and knead together with a little water. Then put dough in small pieces and roll into small balls. Drop balls in soup for 20 minutes, then serve.

Recipe from United Church Women - Fogo Island.

HAM BEAN SOUP

1 ham bone or bacon butt	1 cup dried beans	1/2 tsp. oregano	1/2 tsp. salt
2 cups potatoes cubed	1 onion	1 cup celery,chopped	1 cup diced carrots
1 cup diced turnip	1/4 clove garlic	1/2 tsp. pepper	

Place ham bone in 2 quarts water, onion, salt, pepper, garlic, beans, celery and oregano. Simmer 1 1/2 hours. Add remaining vegetables. Cover 25 to 30 minutes over medium heat. Good with Dough Boys.

"Labrador Cook Book"

NEWFIE PEA SOUP - Soak piece of salt beef or ham bone overnight. Soak dried peas overnight as well. In morning cook both together in fresh water. Add chopped carrots, turnips, and onions. Boil together 20 minutes. Before serving put in whole potatoes. Serve with dumplings.

Recipe from Labrador Cook Book, Happy Valley & Goose Bay, Labrador

SOUP OLD FASHIONED

Get a good shank beef bone with marrow. Cover with water and cook until tender or nearly done, then remove.

Add about 3 carrots, 2 onions, 2 stalks of celery cut up, 1 green pepper diced, 5 or 6 potatoes, 1/8 tsp. summer savory, salt and pepper to taste, 1 med. can of tomatoes, about 1/2 cup barley and boil until cooked. This is a dinner in itself.

Mrs. E.A. Babstock, Corner Brook, Nfld.

FAT BACK & MOLASSES DIP

Fry a half dozen or so strips of fat back pork (we call them 'rashers') in a fry pan. When all of the fat is fried out of the fat back, then pick up the rashers or you can leave them in if you like. Then pour in about a cupful of molasses (more, if for a crowd) and let it sizzle and boil for 2 or 3 minutes in the fry pan.

Then cool slightly and dip good plain white bread or buns into it. Along with a good cup of tea, it makes a quick, easy and nourishing meal.

"I have never seen or heard of this being cooked much at home, or at any other home, but I do know that when men have been working in the woods in winter time and living in camps and cooking for themselves away from home that they used "Dip" quite a lot."

Mrs. Lewis Hollett, Garden Cove, P.B., Nfld.

PLAIN OLD FASHIONED PORK BUNS

4 cups flour   1/3 lb. salt pork, cut in fine cubes   4 1/2 tsp. baking powder
1 cup lukewarm water, or enough to make tea bun consistency.

Put sifted flour & baking powder in mixing bowl. Cut pork in fine cubes, rinse in warm water and partially fry in pan. Cool pork a little & pour pork & fat derived from it into a hollow made in flour. Add lukewarm water mix with hands to resemble tea bun mixture. Make into buns & bake about 1/2 hour or until golden brown.

"The history of this recipe dates back a long long time. It was used by my grandmother and great grandmother. These buns were used mostly for our grandfathers and uncles, when they went for long trips in the interior of the country to hunt caribou. They were also taken in lunch pack when they went on hunting & trapping trips. Many times they were eaten at home by the children for a snack."

Mrs. Alfred Brinston - Garden Cove

OLD FASHION PORK CAKE

1 lb. mince pork   2 cups sugar   2 oz. cinnamon   1 pint boiling water
1 cup molasses   1 oz. nutmeg.   1 lb. raisins   2 tsp. soda
flour to stiffen, (about 2 1/2 cups)

Mince Pork. Pour boiling water over pork. Add raisins, nutmeg, and cinnamon. Put soda in molasses. Add the flour. Bake in moderate oven for 2 hours.

Mrs. Charlotte Osborne - Little Bay East

LOCAL JOKE: A woman was busy one day doing her washing & ironing & getting her meals ready for her family, but somewhere in between she managed to bake a cake. Later on that evening the clergy dropped in for a visit. She happily cut her cake and served it with tea for the clergy. When the minister was about to compliment her on the cake she exclaimed, "O my Lard, I forgot the put the Lord in me cake!"

Mrs. Norma Vey, Hillview, Trinity Bay

MOLASSES BUNS OR JAY BUNS

1/2 cup butter	1 well beaten egg	1 tbsp. milk	1/4 tsp salt
1/2 cup molasses	1/2 cup brown sugar	1 tsp. cinnamon	1 1/2 cups flour
1 cup diced pork	1 tsp. soda		

Cream butter & sugar. Add egg & vanilla and molasses. Sift together dry ingredients with milk. Bake in cup cake pans at 350 F. for 15 - 20 minutes. Raisins may be added if desired.

"These buns proved to be the staple lunch for woodsmen or fishermen. Made with molasses, they did not dry so easily. The pork & molasses provided heat and energy during cold weather - almost a 'must' for hard working Newfoundlanders.

They were also called 'Jay Buns' because the saucy Jay birds often stole them from the hands of the men while eating, or they certainly came in for all the left-overs by the woodsmen."

Mrs. Mable Squires, Blackhead, Conception Bay

MOLASSES BUNS

1/2 cup butter	1 cup molasses	1 tsp. cloves	2 tsp. allspice	2 tsp. ginger
1 cup boiling water	4 tsp. baking soda	1 cup sugar	5 1/2 cups flour	

Mix butter, molasses, sugar & boiling water in a bowl. Add spices & baking soda. Chill in fridge for 20 minutes then shape into buns and bake.

"This recipe came to me from my husband's grandmother, Mrs. William Eddy. Her husband was the first settler to live in North Hr., having moved here from Hollett's Cove, a small fishing cove near Come By Chance."

Mrs. Ann Eddy, North Hr. Plac. Bay

NEWFOUNDLAND WISDOM: "A test of good manners is being able to put up pleasantly with bad ones."

Mrs. Florence Wilkinson-Moores, Topsail

OLD TIME MOLASSES BUNS

2 cups molasses
3 cups flour (more if needed)
1 cup raisins if desired

2 cups pork fat
l cup sugar
pork scrunchions

1 tsp. cloves
2 tsp. baking soda

2 tsp. allspice
1/2 cup hot water

Stir baking soda in hot water. Add this to molasses in large mixing bowl. Stir until foamy. Add other ingredients. Stir well until all the flour is mixed up. Use large mixing spoon to mix real well. If too soft to handle with hands, mix in little extra flour, then pinch off bun size pieces.

Place in pan or pyrex dish well greased side by side. Bake in slow over at 200 F. Use pan of cool water in oven to keep buns from burning. This keeps the heat at low temperature. Cook until done. Make sure heat not too hot as molasses is easy to burn real quick. When buns are cooked, let cool little in pan, then turn out on cake rack and cool more. Place buns in large tin to hold buns a couple days to improve flavour.

"These old time molasses buns were eaten by men working long hours in the woods cutting firewood to burn in their stoves on the hard frosty days. The molasses buns were something to chew on good and hardy to fill their hungry bellies in the winter time. After the firewood was cut down and hauled out, the men would rest for awhile and then light the fire in a hole in the snow. They held the kettle of water and tea over the open flame (or used a green stick cut for that purpose) until it would boil over. They would sit by the warm fire and munch on that big home made molasses bun and drink the black tea until their bellies could hold no more. The men could then work harder than ever. The molasses buns gave them lots of energy to work harder in the woods."
Mrs. Ewart Marshall, Little Bay East, Fortune Bay,

OLD FASHIONED PORK BREAD - Cut into small pieces about 2 cups of salt pork and mix in a bowl with a little salt, 3 cups flour and l pkg. dry yeast. Add just enough water to make a soft dough. Then let rise and bake the same as you would plain bread or buns.

"Mother often used to make this recipe when we were home and we would always have some when we would leave for our trip down the bay to our summer place which took two or three days, according to the weather."
May McLean, North West River, Labrador

SALT PORK BUNS

1 cup finely chopped salt pork	1 1/2 cup water	1/2 cup molasses	1/2 tsp salt
4 cups sifted flour	1/4 cup margarine	8 tsp. baking powder	

Fry out salt pork. Drain well. Sift dry ingredients into a bowl and cut in margarine. Add scrunchions & mix with a fork until the pork is well scattered. Combine molasses & water. Add them to the flour mixture and stir lightly. Roll out on a floured board to 1/2 inch thickness. Cut into desired shapes. Place on floured baking sheet. Bake at 400 F. for 15 minutes.

Mrs. Donald Blake, Barr'd Islands & Mrs. Heber Fifield, Wesleyville.

MORE SALT PORK BUNS

3 cups flour   3 1/2 tsp. baking powder   one piece salt pork   enough cold water to mix them soft.

Put flour, baking powder together. Cut up salt pork into small pieces and fry out till golden brown. Cool and add to mixture. Bake 30 minutes or until golden brown.

"I have been baking these buns for about 10 years. I hope you like them and that they turn out well."   *Mrs. Heber Eddy,- North Harbour, Placentia Bay.*

OLD FASHION PORK BUNS

1/4 lb. salt pork	3 tsp. baking powder	1/2 cup warm water
1/2 pkg. seedless raisins	3 cups flour	1 cup sugar

Cut salt pork in 1/4" squares. Place in fry pan. Fry until golden brown. Combine dry ingredients in bowl. Mix fat and warm water together. Mix well into dry ingredients. Roll into buns & place in pan. Bake 400 F. until golden brown.

"This recipe was given to me by Mrs. Lushman on the South Coast. It has been made and enjoyed for a full century or more. It is enjoyed as much today as ever. The ladies of the South Coast of Nfld. could never hold a party without serving 'Old Fashion Pork Buns'."   *Mrs. Minnie Vincent - Newtown, Nfld.*

SOUR DOUGH STARTER

1 cake yeast   2 cups all purpose flour   2 1/2 cups warm water   1 tblsp. sugar   2 tsp. salt

Dissolve yeast in 1/2 cup warm water to which 1 tbsp. sugar has been added. Let stand 10 minutes. Stir in remaining ingredients. Put in a large crock, cover loosely with a towel and let stand in a warm place (80 to 90 F).

Stir down daily. In 3 or 4 days it will be ready to use. When some starter is withdrawn from the crock, replace it with equal amounts of water and flour each time for re-use in future.

"This is an old recipe used by people many years ago when yeast was scarce. It has been tested by a member of our local U.C.W. and found very good indeed for 'Hotcakes.'"

United Church Women, Pt. Leamington, N.D. Bay

HOTCAKES MADE WITH SOURDOUGH STARTER

1 cup flour   1 egg   1 tsp. soda   1 cup milk
1 cup sourdough starter   1 tblsp. sugar   1/2 tsp. salt   1/2 tbsp. oil

Mix the night before, 1 cup flour and 1 cup milk. Beat. Let stand until until morning then add 1 cup sourdough starter. Beat egg, add sugar, oil, soda & salt. Combine with first mixture. Drop on hot greased griddle, cook until bubbles form then turn to brown other side. Serve with maple syrup or jam.

N. B. - These are good served with bacon or ham or plain if you like pancakes.

United Church Women, Pt. Leamington, N.D. Bay

BOILED CAKE: 2 cups sugar; 1 1/2 cups raisins; 1 cup butter; 3 tsp. spices, 1 1/2 cups warm water & 2 tsp. soda. Boil together for 5 minutes. Let cool. Add 3 cups flour & the soda, nuts & citron if desired. Bake 1 1/2 or 2 hours with slow heat. *Mrs. Ellen Good, Little By East, F. Bay*

MOLASSES BUNS

1 cup molasses
1/2 cup salt pork(fried)

1/2 tsp. baking soda
1 cup boiling water

1/2 tsp. cinnamon
1 1/2 cup flour

First cut up pork in mall pieces, fry out and let cool. Pour boiling water in bowl, add baking soda and let cool. Sift flour & cinnamon together. Combine all ingredients together. Roll out on floured board and cut out.   Bake at 350 F for 15 or 20 minutes.

Mrs. Gertrude Temple, Sunnyside, Nfld..

RAISIN TEA BUNS

3 cups flour
5 tsp. baking powder
1/2 tsp. salt

1 cup milk
1 1/2 cups raisins

1 tsp. nutmeg
1 egg

3/4 cup butter
1/2 cup white sugar

Combine dry ingredients & rub in butter until fine. Combine egg & milk and add to first mixture. Add raisins. Roll lightly. Cut & bake in hot over at 450 F for 15 minutes.

Mrs. Berkley King, St. John's, Nfld.

RAISIN BUNS

3 cups flour
4 tsp baking powder

1/2 cup butter
1 tsp. vanilla

2 cups raisins
1 cup sugar

2 eggs
milk

1/2 tsp. salt

Rub together butter & flour. Add sugar, raisins, baking powder, salt & eggs. Add enough milk to make soft dough. Cut & bake.

M. Beazley, Burin, Nfld.

NEWFOUNDLAND WISDOM: "Two things are bad for the heart;
- running upstairs
- running down people."

Mauguerite Sutton, St. Georges, Nfld.

"Trouting" in May Month

MAY month in Newfoundland _The nets and gear are now in good repair and ready for fishing, but the ice is off the shore and fish not yet come. With the welcome lull comes improved weather and with one accord the Newfoundland families move out to 'ponds' to go 'trouting'.

Bamboo poles and worms are all that is needed to catch a pan full of delicious trout. All the family join in the fun which is usually ended with one of the famous Newfoundland 'scoffs' or cookouts.

POTATO PORK BUNS

6 - 8 potatoes   2 cups flour   1/2 lb salt pork (minced)   5 tsp. baking powder   2 - 3 tbsp. butter

Boil potatoes, drain, then add the butter and minced pork. Mash well. Add the sifted flour and baking powder to make a soft dough. Cut out and bake in hot oven. Serve with hot boiled salt fish.

United Church Women, Pt. Leamington, N.D. Bay

POTATO BISCUITS

1 1/2 cups sifted flour   3 tbsp. shortening   4 tsp. baking powder   1/2 tsp. salt
1 cup cooked potatoes (riced)   1/2 cup cold milk

Sift together dry ingredients, cut in shortening. Lightly mix in cooled riced potatoes. Add cold milk to make a soft dough. Turn out on a floured board, lightly roll and cut into required shapes. Bake on greased sheet at 400F.

"This recipe was taken from an old cook book." U.C.W., Pt. Leamington

SPECIAL OLD TIME RECIPE IN NEWFOUNDLAND

3 cakes hard bread   1 tsp. soda   1 cup molasses   1 tsp. allspice
1 cup fat back pork (finely chopped)

Soak bread overnight. Next morning squeeze dry and crumble. Then add and mix together all other ingredients and boil in same pot with salt meat and cabbage and other vegetables.

"This recipe was used by my mother and as I am 85 years old this recipe is well over one hundred years old."

Mrs. Louise Eddy, North Hr., P. Bay

TEA BUNS

2 cups flour	4 tsp. baking powder	1 egg	pinch of salt
1/2 cup butter	1/3 cup sugar		

Cream butter & sugar. Add beaten egg. Add salt & baking powder to flour. Add to butter mixture with 1/2 cup of milk. Brush the buns with milk before putting in the oven.

D. Moulton, Burin, Newfoundland

NAIN PASTRY

1 lb. flour	1 lb. lard	3 egg yolks	3/4 tsp. salt
3 tbsp. sour cream	3 tbsp. vinegar		

If canned milk is used instead of cream, the vinegar would sour it after being slightly warmed. One lb. of sifted flour measures approx. 3 3/4 cups.

Labrador Cook Book

TRAPPER'S BREAD

3 cups flour	2 pkg. yeast	3 tsp salt	1 tsp. cloves
2 cups brown sugar	1 cup molasses	1 cup currants	1 tsp. cinnamon
2 cups raisins	1 cup melted shortening	2 tsp. nutmeg	

Place currants and raisins in bowl and cover with hot water. Let stand. Put flour in large mixing bowl. Add salt, sugar and spices. Pour in molasses and melted shortening. Mix yeast according to directions. Add risen yeast to mixture and mix well. Add water to dough to make as smooth as plain bread. Remove currants & raisins from water and add to dough, mixing well. Cover bowl. Let rise, then bake.

Labrador Cook Book

"RAMES" - "A skeleton - the bare bones. Applied to a thin man or woman."

E.R. Hann, Wesleyville, Nfld.

METHODIST, OR WESLEYAN BREAD

Dissolve 2 pkg. yeast, 2 tsp. sugar in 1 cup luke warm water. Take 3 cups luke warm water and 3/4 cup molasses and 1/4 cup lard or shortening and 4 tsp. salt.

Add the yeast mixture and six tbsp. sugar. Stir well, then add 12 cups sifted flour, 1 pkg. raisins, 1/4 tsp. grated nutmeg or 2 tsp. caraway seed. Mix with hand and turn out on floured board. Knead well for about 10 to 15 minutes.

Brush with melted shortening and place in pan to rise until double its bulk. Knead down again with greased hands. After this rising, knead again and form into loaves and place into baking pans. Brush top again with melted shortening. Allow to rise again until double its bulk. Bake in 375 F oven about 1 hour. When removed from oven brush top again with melted butter.

'This recipe is tradionally used on Christmas eve with watered boiled salt fish.'

Mrs. Florence Wilkinson-Moores, Topsail.

PORK TOUTONS

4 cups flour	1 cup molasses	1/2 tsp. baking powder	1/2 tsp. baking soda

1 lb. fat pork, (finely chopped or minced)

Mince or chop pork & place in hot water to remove some of the salt. Let stand for 10 minutes. Sift dry ingredients. Remove pork from water & add to molasses. Add flour mixture to molasses mixture, alternately with enough water to make a soft dough. Pat out on floured board and cut into buns. Bake at 400 F for 20 to 25 min.

Mrs Alice Lacey, Wesleyville, B. B., Nfld.

TOUTONS

In the old days bread was put to rise overnight. When white bread had risen ready to go in pans, small pieces the size of an egg were broken off and flattened 1/2 inch thick in the palms of hands and dropped in the frying pan where fat-back cut up had been fried out until pork was crisp. It was browned on both sides and served for a hot breakfast to children leaving for school on a cold winter morning. Hot molasses with a knob of butter melted in it was the choice sauce, but of course, golden syrup or marmalade could be used as desired.

Mrs. Florence Wilkinson-Moores, Topsail

PORK CAKE

(Note: This recipe has been added to the 2nd edition of Fat-Back & Molasses because it is different from all others. It shows how one of the more common recipes has been embellished to further tantalize hungry members in the Newfoundland home.)

1 lb. salt pork	1 pt. boiling water	1 tsp. soda	1 tsp. ginger
4 cups flour	1 cup molasses	1 lb. currants	1 lb. raisins
1/2 lb. citron	1/2 lb. nuts	1 cup jam	1 tsp. cloves
2 cups sugar	2 tsp. nutmeg.	2 tsp. cinnamon	

Pour boiling water over minced pork and add molasses and jam. Sift all dry ingredients. Add fruit and blend well. Bake in a slow oven for 2 1/2 hours. *Mary Driscoll, New Melbourne, Trinity Bay*

GOOD FRIDAY BUNS

Scald 1 cup milk with 1/2 tsp. salt and 1/4 cup sugar. Cool. Dissolve a yeast cake (or 1 pkg. yeast) in half cup warm water and add to milk. Mix in 2 cups sifted flour, beat well and let rise for 2 hours until light and spongy.

Next, fold in three tbsp. melted butter, 2 well beaten eggs, 1/4 tsp. cinnamon, 1/4 tsp. grated nutmeg, 1/4 cup raisins, 2 tbsp. mixed peel and enough flour to make dough stiff enough to handle. Add the flour gradually, keeping dough soft. Knead well and let rise again.

Shape into buns and place in moderate oven. When cool, decorate a cross with icing sugar and milk on top of each bun.

"These were eaten for tea on Good Fridays and Easter morning breakfast. This recipe was given to the writer by Mrs. Ralph Wood, wife of Ralph Wood who was for many years the Head Master of Bishop Field College." *Mrs. Florence Wilkinson-Moores, Topsail*

PLIM - "To make a barrel or keg tight by filling it with water or standing it in running water to soak."
E R. Hann, Wesleyville , B. B, Nfld..

DAMPER DOGS

"For 'Damper Dogs' we used to get some little pieces of bread dough when mother made her regular batch of home-made bread and flatten them out. After wiping off the top of the old 'Waterloo' with a clean cloth or paper, we would then put the pieces of dough on the edge of the stove and let them brown to a lovely crust on both sides. They would always rise up or swell in size about double the original piece of dough. Sometimes when the stove was not too hot, we would move the bread dough farther in on the damper, hence the name 'Damper dogs'. Sometimes we also made damper buns with ordinary baking powder biscuit dough."   Mrs. Lewis Hollett, Garden Cove, P. Bay, Nfld.

SCOTCH CURRANT BUN (GLENORCHY)

1 lb. flour	1 lb. sugar	1/4 lb. orange peel	1/4 lb. almonds
1 cup buttermilk	2 lbs. currants	2 lbs. raisins	2 tsp. ginger
1/3 1 tsp. black pepper	2 tsp. cinnamon	2 tsp. Jamaican pepper	1 tsp. baking soda
1 tsp. cream of tartar			

(Take 1 1/2 pounds flour, 1/4 lb. butter, 1/2 tsp. baking powder for sheet of pastry which encloses the bun). The fruit must be carefully prepared — stone raisins, clean currants, blanch almonds, cut orange peel. Put all fruit, flour, sugar and spices in big basin, set aside and make pastry, using quantities given above. Rub butter in flour with baking powder, making into stiff dough with water. Roll pastry thin. Grease tin; line with pastry, keeping piece for top of bun. Now pour milk in flour and mix, also fruit, and mix with hand. It must be moist. Pour into tin and put on top sheet. Dot with fork and bake 3 hours in moderate oven.

"Taken from Cook Book 80 years old - The New Cook Book".   Mrs. Eileen Thistle, Corner Brook, Nfld.

"DUFF DAY" - "Figged Duff was mostly served on Thursdays, so Thursday became known as Duff Day."
                              Mrs. Pearl Hatfield, Collins Cove

POTATO SALAD

5 large potatoes (diced)   2 boiled eggs (diced)   salad dressing   1 apple, (diced)
1 tin mixed vegetables

Mix ingredients with salad dressing & sprinkle over with paprika.

Louise Decker - Joe Batt's Arm

COTTAGE CHEESE

1 gallon sweet skim milk   1/8 junket tablet   4 tsp. cold water   1 tsp. salt.
3/4 cup clean sour milk

Stir sour milk into sweet milk. Place vessel in hot water and raise temperature to almost luke-warm. Remove and set where it is to remain until clabbered. Dissolve junket tablet in water and stir it in. Cover the vessel with a cloth and leave it where it will be lukewarm for 12 to 16 hours, or until there is a slight whey on the top. Drain through a cotton cloth. When well drained work in salt.

Mrs. Tom Best - Fogo

SWEET PICKLES

1 large tin tomatoes   3 large onions (sliced)   3 large apples (sliced)   1 tsp. salt.
1 cup white sugar   1 tbsp. mixed spices   1cup vinegar

Mix above ingredients together and boil for 35 minutes.

United Church Women - Fogo Island.

DILL PICKLES

Use 6 qt. basket of cucumbers about 3 or 4 inches long. Wash and pack in clean jars. You put a nice sized flower of dill at the bottom and top, enough garlic to taste (optional) about 1 tsp. mixed spices on top. Now you make your brine.

1 cup salt (course)	2 cups white vinegar	6 cups water

Bring to a boil, then pour over cucumbers in jars. Seal. Let sit for a couple of weeks before you use them.

"I read your cook book while visiting my daughter-in-law (who is from Newfoundland) and thought what a good cook book it is."

Mrs. G. Iwanonkiw, Thunder Bay, Ontario

BEAN SALAD

1 sm. tin green beans	1 sm. tin yellow beans	1 sm. tin kidney beans	1 tsp. pepper
2 sticks celery (cut up)	1 onion (sliced in rings)	2/3 cup vinegar	1 tsp. salt
1/2 cup sugar	1/2 cup salad oil (not corn)		

Drain all beans and mix everything together. Let stand in fridge 3 hours.

Mrs. Rosalind Fraser, Sudbury, Ont. (Bishop's Falls)

MACARONI SALAD

1 lb. macaroni (cooked and rinsed in cold water). Drain. Add - 1 sm. tin green peas, 1 cup cheese cut in cubes, 1 tin tuna or ham, 1 onion (chopped), 1 stalk celery (chopped). Add salad dressing to taste.

Mrs. Rosalind Fraser, Sudbury, Ont. (Bishop's Falls)

BEET AND APPLE SALAD

1 pkg. lemon gelatin	1 tbsp. lemon juice	3/4 cup chopped beets	1 tsp. salt
1 cup boiling water	1/2 cup chopped apple	1 cup beet juice	1/8 tsp. pepper

Soften gelatin in boiling water. Add beet & lemon juice, salt & pepper. Chill until partially set. Fold in beets & apple. Pour into mold & allow to set until firm.

Mrs. Stella Decker - Joe Batt's Arm

CABBAGE AND APPLE SALAD

1 pkg. lemon jello	1/2 tsp. salt	1 pint hot water	4 tsp. vinegar
1 cup shredded cabbage	1/4 cup chopped sweet pickles	1 cup diced apples	

Dissolve jello in hot water. Add vinegar and salt. Chill until slightly thickened. Fold in cabbage, apples & pickles. Chill until firm. Serve on crisp lettuce.

United Church Women - Seldom Come By

POTATO SALAD

2 cups freshly boiled potatoes	1/8 tsp. pepper	3 tblsp. olive oil	1 tsp. salt
few drops onion juice	1 tbsp. vinegar	1 tbsp. finely minced parsley	

Cut potatoes in 3/4 inch cubes. Add seasoning, then olive oil, only what the potatoes will absorb, then add vinegar & mix carefully until it is absorbed. Mound on a bed of lettuce in a shallow dish. Egg yolks make an attractive garnish if put through a ricer. Tomatoes cut in eighths added to potato salad make a pleasant variation.

Mrs. Parmenas Wells - Fogo

PINEAPPLE JELLIED SALAD

1 pkg. lemon jelly	1 tin crushed pineapple (drained)	2 tablespoons mayonaise
1 cup grated raw carrot	1 cup grated cabbage	1 tsp. vinegar & pinch of salt

Set jelly, grate carrot and cabbage. When jelly is almost set add 1 tspn. vinegar & pinch of salt. Add grated carrot & cabbage & pineapple. Mix well together, add salad dressing. but in refrigerator to set.

Mrs. B..M. Penny - Little Seldom Come By

BEET SALAD

Mix 1 envelope gelatine with 1 1/2 cups lukewarm water. Set over slow heat and stir until clear. Set aside and cool. Add 2 cups diced beet, 1 diced apple, 1/2 cup shredded cabbage, pinch of salt, 1 teaspoon vinegar and 1/4 cup sugar. Mix together. When gelatine is set, mix with beet mixture.

Mrs. R. E. Holmes - Seldom Come By

DANDELION GREES

Pick over the greens to remove all dirt and spoilage. Wash thoroughly. Put in a saucepan containing just enough water to prevent burning. Add a mall amount of salt pork. Cook until tender. All greens may be cooked this way.

Mrs. Tom Best - Fogo

SANDWICHES

Combine 1/2 cup ground ham, 1 chopped hard boiled egg, 1/4 cup salad dressing or mayonnaise, 2 tbsp. chopped sweet pickle & 1 tsp. of prepared mustard.

United Church Women - Fogo Island.

JUNE begins with the Lobster. Some of the fishermen batch together in one of their 'tilts' built along the shore, a small shack with bunks and a 'bogie'. From here they leave early each morning to pull up their lobster pots. Every pot is weighted down with heavy rocks, so imagine yourself pulling up and letting down two or three hundred of those before the day's end and you will understand why the men enjoy a good 'scoff' before turning in at night. This particular 'tilt' in the picture above is situated at Shoal Bay, Fogo Island, and has been the point of origin for many scrumptious lobster dinners shipped via air freight to the Mainland centres.

CURRIED SALT COD SALAD

1 lb. cooked salt cod
1/2 cup raisins
1 1/2 tsp. curry Powder

1 tbsp. lemon juice
1 unpeeled red apple, diced
1/2 cup salad dressing

1/2 cup chopped onions
1 cup diced celery & leaves

Flake salt cod. Sprinkle lemon juice over diced apples. Combine apples, celery, raisins and onions. Add salt cod. Mix curry powder and salad dressing. Combine with mixture and toss lightly, garnish with lettuce and red pimento.

Ellen Keats - Barr'd Islands

NEWFOUNDLAND LOBSTER SALAD

3 freshly boiled lobsters (shelled)
3 hard cooked eggs, chopped

1/2 tsp. salt, few grains pepper
1/2 cup sweet pickles (chopped)

1 small onion, finely minced
1/2 cup mayonnaise

Cut lobster into bite size pieces. Add other ingredients and toss together. Serve on lettuce leaves.

Mx. Margaret Freake - Joe Batt's Arm

APPLE PICKLES

1 doz. apples (med. size)
2 tsp. pickling spices (tied in thin cloth)

2 1/2 lbs. onions

1 large tin tomatoes
1 pint white vinegar

1 1/4 lbs. brown sugar

Cook until tender.

Mrs. Eunice Budgell, Lewisporte, Nfld.

TOMATO PICKLES

| 1 tin tomatoes, large | 4 apples | 1 cup vinegar | 1 tsp. allspice |
| 2 or 3 onions | 1 tsp. salt | 1 cup sugar | |

Put all in pan together and boil 3/4 or 1 hour.

Mrs. Alex Hynes - Stag Harbour

TOMATO PICKLES

| 1 large tin tomatoes | 3 large apples | 1/2 cup white vinegar | 1/2 tsp. salt |
| 2 large onions | 1 cup sugar | | |

Boil all together for 35 minutes or until onions are well cooked.

Mrs. Sarah Brown - Joe Batt's Arm

MY MOTHER'S FAVOURITE PICKLE

One quart raw cabbage chopped fine; one quart boiled beets chopped fine; two cups of sugar, one tbs. salt, one tsp. black pepper, 1/4 tsp. red pepper, one teacup grated horse-radish. Cover with cold vinegar & keep from the air.

Mrs. Parmenas Wells - Fogo

FAREWELL KISS

"A person from the congregation went to church one Sunday afternoon for a special service and when the evening offering was taken, he took a fifty cent piece from his pocket and kissed it goodbye. And it happened shortly after that there were no more old fifty cent pieces made."

Mrs. Florence Bursey, New Melbourne, T. Bay

RHUBARB RELISH

2 qts. rhubarb	1 tsp. spice	1/4 tsp. pepper	2 tsp. cinnamon
1 qt. vinegar (diluted)	2 qts. onions	1 tsp. cloves	1 lb. brown sugar

Cut rhubarb & onions in small pieces. Soak in salt overnight. Wash and strain. Put together. Let simmer for 3 hours with cover half off.

Mrs. Melvin Holmes - Seldom Come By

MUSTARD PICKLES

2 qts. chopped onions	2 qts. cabbage

Make brine of 4 pints of water & 1 pint of salt. Pour over vegetables & let stand 24 hours. Drain & cover with fresh water. Mix together 1 cup flour with 6 tsp. dry mustard, 1 tsp, turmeric powder. Add enough vinegar to make small batter. Add 2 cups sugar & enough vinegar to make 2 quarts. Heat mixture in double boiler. Add vegetables & cook only until heated through.

Mrs. Bride Sheppard - Stag Harbour

PICKLED BEETS

Boil small beets until tender. Skin them. For each quart of beets, allow 1 1/2 cups of brown sugar, 1 tsp. salt, 3/4 cup table vinegar and 3/4 cup water in which beets were boiled. Heat beets in this mixture until it boils. Fill hot sterilized jars & seal.

Mrs. Margaret Freake - Joe Batt's Arm Arm

WEATHER LORE: "When distant hills appear near,
  Rainy weather is coming."

Annie Hodder, Collins Cove, Burin

MUSTARD PICKLES

10 lb. onions	3 tbsp. turmeric	2 qts. vinegar
1 cup flour	3 tbsp. mustard	2 cups sugar

Cut onions in large pieces & soak overnight in 3/4 cup salt. Cover with cool water & let stand until morning. Place on stove & bring to a boiling point. Strain off dry as possible. Add the remainder ingredients. Boil one hour or little longer if necessary. Cool & bottle. *Mrs. W. J. Goodland - Joe Batt's Arm*

CABBAGE PICKLES

2 qts. cabbage	1 cup gran. sugar	1 tbsp. tumeric powder	1 tsp. salt
2 qts. onions	1 tbsp. dry mustard	1 tbsp. curry powder	1 qt. vinegar
1/2 cup flour	1 cup water		

Chop cabbage & onion until fine. Add vinegar & boil 15 minutes. Add salt & sugar. Mix seasonings with the flour & add water to make a paste. Stir flour paste into the boiling pickles & boil for 15 minutes more. Bottle while hot. *Myrtice Pomeroy - Fogo*

CARROT PICKLES

3 lbs. onions	1 lb. carrots	1 pt. vinegar	2 lbs. sugar	1/2 head cabbage

Cook onions, carrot and cabbage until tender, adding salt to taste, then thicken with the following:

6 tblsp. mustard	1/2 cup sugar	1 cup flour	1 tblsp. turmeric mixed with one cup vinegar & water.

Mrs. Bernice Hynes - Stag Harbour

PARTRIDGEBERRY PICKLES

1 quart Partridgeberries	1 cup vinegar	pinch of salt	sugar to taste
1 inch onions (cut up fine)	1 tsp. allspice		

Bring above ingredients to boil until jelled.

Louise Decker - Joe Batt's Arm

RHUBARB PICKLES

Add together 1 quart rhubarb, 1 quart onions & 1 pint vinegar & boil for twenty minutes. Then add 1 1/2 lb. of brown sugar, 1 tsp. cinnamon, 1 tsp. spice, 1 tsp. cloves, 1 tsp. salt & 1 tsp. pepper. Cook for 1 1/4 hours.

Nora Leyte - Fog0

RHUBARB PICKLES

4 cups rhubarb	1 cup vinegar	2 tsp. allspice	2 tsp. salt
1 lb. onions	1 tsp. cloves	1 tsp. cinnamon	1 lb. sugar

Boil all ingredients for one hour.

Mrs. W.J. Goodland - Joe Batt's Arm

APPLE PICKLES

1 dozen apples	1 can tomatoes	1 pint vinegar	spices
2 1/2 lbs. onions	1 1/2 lb. brown sugar		

Boil until tender.

Nora Leyte - Fogo

MOLASSES PUDDING

2 1/2 cups flour	1/2 cup molasses	1 cup sugar	1 tbsp. vanilla
1/2 cup milk	1/2 pkg. raisins	3 tsp. soda	1/4 cup hot water
2 tsp. mixed spice	2 tsp. ginger	1/2 cup butter	

Sift together flour, spice & ginger. Cream together butter & sugar. Add molasses. Mix well, then add vanilla, milk & raisins. Blend together well. Put the 3 tsp. soda in 1/4 cup hot water & add to above mixture. Combine sifted ingredients with liquid mixture. Put into wet pudding bag. Boil constantly for 3 hours.

"The history of the above recipe is not really well known to me, but I do know that it is quite old. It was used on many occasions, like at church suppers & bazaars. It was served to the people for dessert after a hot supper. Usually a hot sauce was poured over it. Our grandmother and great grandmothers served it numerous times to their families and it certainly was enjoyed by all and helped keep them healthy and happy."

Mrs. Eric Williams, Garden Cove, P.S.

STEAM PUDDING

1 cup butter	1 cup raisins	1 egg and pinch of salt	2 tsp. baking powder
1 cup sugar	1 1/2cups flour		

Combine butter and sugar, add egg and raisins, flour and baking powder and beat well and place in a pudding steamer and place on stove for 1 hour. Serve hot with sauce.

"Called steam pudding because it was steamed." *Mx. Mrs. Eli Wareham, Garden Cove.*

BREAD PUDDING: Heat 4 cups milk & add 4 tbsp. butter, 1/2 cup sugar, 1/2 tsp salt, 1 tsp. vanilla and 1/2 cup raisins. Beat and stir up 3 eggs. Fold in 4 cups bread cut in cubes. Pour into a buttered pan. Sprinkle with cinnamon or nutmeg. Steam for 40 - 50 minutes or until knife comes out clean, when inserted near centre of pudding.

Mrs. Hilda Stacey, Garden Cove.

STEAMED MOLASSES PUDDING

1 egg	1/2 cup water	1 cup raisins or currants	1 tsp. soda
3/4 cup molasses	1 1/2 cups flour	2 tbsp. melted fat	1/2 tsp. salt

Beat egg & add molasses. Dissolve soda in water & stir into egg mixture. Sift flour & salt, add and beat thoroughly. Dredge raisins in flour & stir in lightly. Add fat. Fill greased mold 3/4 full. Cover closely & steam 1 1/4 to 1 1/2 hours. Serve hot with sauce.

SAUCE FOR STEAMED MOLASSES PUDDING: Stir 1 cup brown sugar and 1 cup of light cream(milk) together in saucepan until sugar is dissolved. Set over low heat. Add 1/4 cup butter and cook, stirring often until mixture boils. Remove from heat and stir in 1/4 cup brandy. Serve while hot.

QUICK APPLE PUDDING

2 tbsp. butter	6 tbsp. milk	1 cup chopped apples	1 cup sifted flour
1/4 cup sugar	1/2 tsp salt	1 tsp. baking powder	

Cream butter & sugar. Sift dry ingredients and stir in apples. Add this to creamed mixture with milk. Pour into 2 qt. dish.

SAUCE FOR QUICK APPLE PUDDING: Combine 1 cup brown sugar, 1 tbsp. butter and a few grains of salt together. Add 1 1/2 cups boiling water and stir until sugar dissolves. Add 1 tsp. vanilla and mix. Pour sauce over above batter and bake at 400 F. for 30 to 35 minutes.

Mrs. Cyril Mahaney, Fogo, Nfld.

AMERICAN ICE CREAM: Make a soft custard using 2 eggs, 1/8 tsp. salt and 1 cup sugar mixed with 2 1/2 cups of milk. When cool, add 4 cups cream and 1 tsp. vanilla. Freeze mixture, stirring slowly until firm.

United Church Women, Fogo Island, Nfld.

SAILOR'S DUFF

1/4 cup shortening	1/4 cup brown sugar	1 egg	pinch of salt
1/2 cup molasses	2 tbsp. canned milk	1/2 cups flour	1/2 tsp. vanilla
1/2 tsp. soda dissolved in 1 tbsp.boiling water		1 tsp. baking powder	

Cream shortening and sugar, add egg, then molasses, milk and other ingredients. Mix well. Then add 1/2 cup boiling water, mix in well. You can add 1/2 tsp. of any spices, also 1 cup of raisins. Steam 2 hours.

"This recipe was passed down from my great grandmotherwho lived her life in Chimney Cove, where she was known to everyone as Granny Breton. She was a midwife." Marguerite Sutton, St. Georges

GRANDMOTHER'S DELICIOUS GINGERBREAD

2 eggs	1 cup brown sugar	1 cup molasses	allspice or cloves
1/2 cup shortening	2 3/4 cups flour	1/2 tsp. salt	1 tsp. ginger
1 cup buttermilk (or semi-sour or plain milk)		2 tsp. soda	1 tsp cinnamon

Beat the eggs, add sugar, mix well. Add molasses. Melt shortening & mix together. Sift flour, salt, ginger & cinnamon & spices and then add alternately with cupful of buttermilk. Last add soda dissolved in warm water. Bake in moderate oven for 25 or 30 minutes.

"We received this recipe from Brantford, Ontario, about 50 or more years ago, and it is all that its name implies. It has been used very much in our family and in a variety of ways, such as made up into gingerbread buns and patty-buns (or muffins, as they would more likely be called now). It was a real favourite in years gone by at socials and church teas and so on. I got it from my husband's mother about 42 years ago. It was taken from Miss Olive Allen's book of tested recipes. My mother-in-law would be 103 years old now if living and I know that I am safe in saying that she brought many a smile of satisfaction to her family's table when she came from the old-fashioned pantry with a platter of this steaming gingerbread served with butter."

Mrs. Lewis Hollet, Garden Cove, P. Bay

DARK SUET PUDDING

1/2 cup suet	3/4 tsp. baking powder	1/2 cup molasses	raisins or currants
1 1/2 cups flour	1 tsp. baking soda	1/2 cup milk	2 tsp. spice
(add chopped nuts for Christmas pudding)		1/2 tsp. salt	

Cut up fat in very small pieces. Rub it through flour. Mix in all the dry ingredients. Add molasses and milk. Stir until well mixed. Add fruit and flavouring if desired. Put into a greased bowl or pudding steamer. Steam for 2 1/2 hours. Serve hot.

Sauce: 1/2 cup brown sugar, 2 tsp. flour & 1 tbsp. butter. Mix sugar & flour well in a small saucepan. Add butter. Stir in 1 1/2 cups boiling water. Place on stove & boil for a few minutes. Add 1 tsp. vanilla or lemon flavouring before serving.

"The above recipe makes a very delicious pudding. It was given to me by a dear friend who had received it from her mother. It is a very old Newfoundland recipe. I have made this pudding several times and received some very good comments about it. If you try it I am sure you will be asked to serve it again."
                                                                    Mrs. John Howell, Garden Cove, P.B.

HARD BREAD PUDDING

4 cakes hard bread	1/4 lb. salt pork	1 tsp. pepper	1 onion

Soak bread overnight. Strain & mash. Chop onion fine and add to mashed bread. Add pepper. Put in pudding bag and tie tightly. Boil with Jiggs dinner for 2 hours. Serve with molasses or corn syrup if used for dessert.

"A substantial meal for men returning home after a hard day's work, as they often referred to it as a 'standby' or as some put it, 'It stayed with you.' It's not like soup, which makes you feel hungry shortly after drinking it."
                                                                    Mrs. Mabel Squires, Blackhead U.C.W. Pres.

Lorie Jesperson — TrapBoat

The Trap Skiff is a familiar sight in JULY month, but not with a fishermen who has his hands in his pockets. Little did the thirteen year old artist realize that she was capturing one of the seafaring traditions of Canada's newest province. When one crew has more fish in its trap than their skiff can hold, another crew is invited to load up their boat with the overflow. In the scene above, the fisherman on the right had just boarded the skiff to survey the situation. In a few minutes he would be lending his hands to the task and then later load his own boat awaiting in the background.

BLUEBERRY COBBLER

2 cups blueberries	1 tsp. baking powder	1/2 cup sugar	1/2 tsp. vanilla
4 tbsp. sugar	2 tsp. butter	1 egg, well beaten	1 cup flour
1/2 tsp. salt	1/4 cup milk		

Put the berries into a baking dish, sprinkle with the 4 tbsp. sugar. Sift remaining dry ingredients. Add egg, milk and melted butter, stirring just enough to combine. Spread batter over blueberries and bake in a moderate oven 350 F. about 40 minutes. Serve from baking dish or invert on platter. Serve with plain or whipped cream.

Mrs. Minnie Penney - Seldom Come By

OLD FASHIONED SULTANA CAKE

3 1/2 cups flour	4 eggs	1/2 tsp. baking powder
3/4 lb. butter	1 tsp. vanilla	1 cup milk
2 cups sugar	1/4 tsp. salt	(no raisins used)

Cream butter & sugar. Add eggs one at a time. Sift dry ingredients and add to creamed mixture. Add vanilla & milk. Mix well. Bake in large pan for 2 1/2 hours.

"This cake recipe is used when mothers have been very busy with everyday chores. They find it very easy to mix and bake and inexpensive as well. Of course, it has been connected with mothers, daughters and even grandchildren and friends, so each generation have found this recipe to be of good value."

Mrs. Florence Bursey, New Melbourne, T. Bay

POOR MAN'S PUDDING

Boil 2 cups water. Add 1 cup brown sugar, 1 tbsp margarine, 1 tsp. vanilla. Mix together 1/2 cup white sugar, 1 cup flour, 1 tsp. baking powder, 1/2 cup milk.

Put first mixture in casserole dish. Drop second mixture by teaspoon onto first mixture. Bake 350 F. for 30 minutes.

Mrs. Rosalind Fraser, Sudbury, Ont. (Bishop's Falls)

CHRISTMAS STEAM PUDDING

1/2 lb. raisins	1/2 lb. figs	1/2 lb. mixed fruit	1 cup butter (1/2 lb)
4 eggs well beaten	1 tsp. baking powder	1/2 lb. dates	2 1/2 cups flour
1/2 cup brown sugar	1 cup Karo	1/4 cup brandy	1 tsp. suet
1 tsp. cinnamon	1 tsp. all spice	1/2 tsp. cloves	1/2 tsp. nutmeg

Sift together all dry ingredients then cream butter and sugar well. Add Karo. Mix well. Add 1 cup dry ingredients to batter and mix till smooth. Add eggs beat well. Add fruit which has been soaked in brandy over night. Fold in remaining flour mixture.
Steam 4 1/2 hours in 2 quart pudding mold.

Mrs. B. Dyke

HARD TIMES PUDDING

1 1/2 cups flour	1 tsp. cream tartar	2 cups currants	1/2 pint molasses
1 tsp. magic soda	1 tsp. mixed spice	1 tbsp. melted butter	1/4 tsp. salt
1 cup raisins	1/2 pint cold water		

Sift together flour, cream of tartar, salt and spice. Add fruit and mix well. Add soda to molasses, then melted butter and cold water. Add this to the first mixture. Beat into a smooth batter and steam for 2 hours.

METHODIST BREAD — An old name in Newfoundland for raisin bread.

E.R. Hann, Wesleyville, B.B., Nfld.

BOILED APPLE PUDDING

5 or 6 apples	2 tbsp. brown sugar	1/2 lb. butter	cinnamon
6 or 8 potatoes	flour		

Peel & quarter apples and put in cold water. Make a crust of 6 to 8 potatoes boiled & mashed. Add butter rubbed well into potatoes and as much flour & cold water as required to make a stiff paste. Roll out about 1 inch thick.

Dip the pudding cloth into boiling water, lay it over a large bowl and put the crust into it. Take apples from water and place half of them in crust. Sprinkle with cinnamon and 1 tsp. brown sugar. Put in the remainder of apples then tie cloth up on top and place into pot of boiling water. Turn frequently in the pot and boil for about 3 hours.

"According to information I received, this recipe was copied from a cookbook published in 1858. It seemed to be very popular in our grandparents' day. The suggestion was made that berries could be used instead of apples and it was somtimes known as 'Berry Pig'." Anna Loughlin, North Hr. Plac. Bay.

BREAD PUDDING

2 cups water	1/4 cup sugar	1/2 cup flour

1/2 doz. slices stale bread and crusts, according to size pudding needed.

Soak stale bread crusts in 2 cups water. Squeeze out all water possible. Mix melted butter (1/4 lb) through bread and sugar. Add flour to make bread firmer to handle. Put in pudding cloth and tie tightly. Place in pot with other vegetables. Boil about 18 - 25 minutes. Serve with boiled molasses or jam.

"This recipe has been used for years by my mother & mother-in-law and even today we all love it, especially my son who prefers to eat it with milk and sugar. No doubt it has been used hundreds of years ago. A wonderful way to use left over bread." Sophie C. Way, Newtown, B.Bay, Nfld.

OLD FASHIONED FIGGED DUFF

3 cups bread crumbs	1 cup raisins	1/4 cup melted butter	1 tsp. soda
1 tsp. each ginger, allspice, & cinnamon	1 tbsp. hot water	1/2 cup flour	3 tbsp. molasses
	1/2 cup brown sugar		

Soak bread in water for a few minutes. Squeeze out water (measure without pressing down). Combine bread & raisins, sugar, salt, spices & mix with a fork. Add molasses, melted butter & soda which has been dissolved in hot water. Add flour & mix well. Pour into dampened pudding bag. Cook with Jigg's dinner for one hour.

"This recipe has been given to us by our older Newfoundland folk who selected their own ingredients because they were skilful cooks. This recipe can br rolled to make molasses buns or put in a baking pan for a molasses cake; bake at own judgement. The recipe is an old Newfoundland favourite."
Submitted by Mrs. Velmore Stacey, Garden Cove, Mable Squires, Blackhead; Pearl Hatfield, Burin; Ruby Loder, North Harbour; and Mrs. Lloyd G. Hann of Wesleyville.

PORK BANG BELLY

2 cups molasses	1 tsp. baking soda	1 tsp. allspice	1 lb. salt pork
4 cups flour	1 tsp. nutmeg		

Heat molasses on stove. Cut pork in small cubes & fry. Add to molasses while hot. Dissolve soda in 1/4 cup boiling water. Add spices to flour. Mix all together. Grease pan and lay rind of pork in bottom. Bake one hour in shallow pan. Eat while warm.
Annie Hodder, Burin - Collins Cove

NEWFOUNDAND SAYINGS: "He was up in the States for a spurt."
'Up in the States' meaning to Mainlanders 'down in the States' and a 'spurt' meaning 'active work for a short duration.'
United Church Women, Swift Current

FIGGIDY DUFF WITH MOLASSES COADY

2 cups bread crumbs	1 cup raisins	1/2 cup molasses	1 tsp. ginger
1 tsp. allspice	1 tsp. cinnamon	1/4 cup melted butter	1 tbsp. hot water
1/4 tsp. salt	1/2 cup flour	1 tsp. baking soda	

Soak stale bread in water for a few minutes. Squeeze out water and measure. Combine crumbs, raisins and molasses, salt, spices and mix with a fork. Add melted butter and baking soda which has been dissolved in hot water. Add flour and mix well. Pour into a pudding bag or greased mould and steam for 2 hours. Serve with molasses coady.

For Molasses Coady - boil for 10 minutes: 1 cup molasses, 1/4 cup water, 3 tbsp. butter and 1 tbsp. vinegar. Spoon over figgidy duff.

"This recipe was used by my mother which was passed to her by her mother, who was 92 years old when she died and she used it on the Labrador while cooking for ten men and then she used it for her family when she married and now I use it for my family." Mrs. Helen Sheppard, Carbonear, South

LASSY COADY DUMPLINGS

For the Dumplings:

	1 1/2 cups all purpose flour	3 tsp. baking powder
1 1/2 tbsp. chilled shortening	2/3 cup cold water or milk	1/2 tsp salt

Mix dry ingredients together, cut in shortening finely, make a well and add water or milk. Mix lightly with a fork, drop dough by spoonfuls over hot stew or hot vegetables, cover closely and simmer 15 minutes. (Never lift the cover).

For the Coady: 1 1/2 to 2 cups molasses.

Put molasses into saucepan, bring to a boil, serve as sauce over hot dumplings.

"This is a family recipe handed down from generation to generation, usually used as a second course when molasses sauce is used. Sometimes dumplings are served without sauce with hot vegetables, especially in spring when there is a shortage of vegetables." Mrs. Jacob Best, Wesleyville, B.B. Nfld.

BAKED RICE PUDDING

1/2 cup sugar	1/2 cup uncooked rice	6 cups water
1 1/2 cups skim milk powder	1 tsp. salt	1/4 cups raisins

Wash rice. Put in large baking dish. Add all ingredients but raisins. Bake in oven at 325 F. for 1 1/2 hours. Stir in raisins and bake another 1/2 hour.

SOUTHERN RICE PUDDING

1 cup uncooked rice	1 cup sugar	1/4 tbsp. cinnamon	dash mace or nutmeg
4 cups milk	4 eggs	2 tbsp. butter or marg.	grated rind 1 lemon

Soak rice in 2 cups of milk for 2 hours. Add remaining milk to rice and cook for 20 minutes over low heat. Set aside. Place butter in a 2 quart casserole and work in sugar until soft. Beat eggs and mix with flavouring spices. Mix rice, butter mixture and egg mixture together. Pour into pan and bake 45 minutes at 350 F.

PARTRIDGEBERRY COTTAGE PUDDING

1 3/4 cups sifted flour	1/4 cup shortening	1 tsp. vanilla	2 1/2 tsp. baking pwdr.
1 cup sugar	2/3 cup milk	1/2 tsp. salt	1 cup partridgeberries
1 egg			

Sift flour, baking powder and salt together. Alternately add flour and milk to sugar mixture, beating after each addition until smooth. Add berries and mix lightly. Pour into 8" sq. greased pan and bake in moderate oven at 350 F. for 30 - 40 minutes. Serve with lemon sauce. Serves six.

RICE PUDDING

Bring 2/3 cup water and 1/4 tsp. salt to boil. Stir in 3/4 cup rice. Remove from heat and let stand 5 minutes. Put 1/4 cup milk and 1 beaten egg yolk in. Add 1/3 cup sugar, 1/3 cup raisins, 1/8 tsp. cinnamon, 1/8 tsp. nutmeg and 1/8 tsp. butter. Take from heat & let stand for 1 hour. Stir just before serving. Serve warm or cool. (serves 4)

Mrs. Alvie Brown - Joe Arm, Nfld.

MOM'S APPLE PUDDING

Make apple jam or use a large size tin of apple pie filling, sweeten to taste and put it in a casserole dish. The jam or filling must be hot. Then:

1 1/2 cups flour	1/3 cup sugar	3 tsp. baking powder	1/4 tsp salt
1/3 cup butter	2/3 cup water		

Sift dry ingredients together into the mixing bowl, rub in the butter well, add water and stir well. Drop by the spoonful into the hot jam and bake until nicely browned at 350 F. Partridgeberry or blue berry jam could also be used. After serving, pour a little milk over the pudding, if desired.

"When we were young, what we liked best about Friday's fish dinner was Mom's apple pudding."

'LASSIE JAM TARTS

Melt 1 cup shortening; add 1 cup molasses add 1 tsp. all spice. Dissolve 1 tsp. soda in 1/2 cup hot water and mix all together. Then add 2 cups flour or enough to make a soft pastry. Press firmly in pie tin and fill with partridgeberry jam. Cut the remaining pastry in strips and criss-cross across tart. Bake in 350 F. oven until pastry is done.

"When the 'Lassie Jam Tart' has cooled, stand well back while your children come runniing for their piece."

Mrs. Stanley Pope, Fogo

SOFT CUSTARD

3 eggs or 6 yolks	2 cups hot milk	1/4 cup sugar	1/4 tsp. salt	1/2 tsp. vanilla

Beat eggs only enough to blend. Add sugar & salt & mix well. Pour on hot milk gradually, stirring constantly. Cook with constant stirring over hot, not boiling, water, until the mixture coats the spoon. (about 7 min.) Strain, chill & add flavouring. Serves 4. If custard curdles with overcooking, beat with an egg beater. This will restore the smoothness.

BAKEAPPLE CRUMBLES

Boil 1 quart bakeapples in water until soft and thick. Add sugar to sweeten.

2 cups flour	1 cup butter	2 cups rolled oats	2 tsp. cinnamon
1 cup sugar			

Combine all the above, cover the bottom of a greased pan with half above mixture. Cover with bakeapple mixture and then put rest of the ingredients on top of bakeapple. Bake until brown.

"Labrador Cook Book'

APPLE CRUMBLE

4 cups sliced peeled apples	1/4 cup butter	1/4 tsp. salt	3/4 cup brown sugar
1/2 cup rolled oats	1/4 cup flour	3 to 4 tbsp. sugar cinnamon	

Place apple slices in buttered shallow baking dish and sprinkle with sugar and cinnamon. Beat butter until creamy, beat in brown sugar, add flour, rolled oats and salt. Blend together well. Sprinkle over apples. Bake in moderately hot oven 375 F for about 40 minutes or until fruit is soft and top is golden brown. Serve warm with thick cream or whipped cream.

United Church Women - Fogo Island

CHERRY OAT CRUMBLE

3/4 cup brown sugar	1/3 cup soft butter	1 tsp. flavouring	1/2 cup flour
3/4 tsp. cinnamon	1/2 cup rolled oats	20 oz. can cherry pie filling	3/4 tsp. nutmeg

Blend ingredients till crumbly in a baking dish. Put one can pie filling and add flavouring. Sprinkle crumb mixture on top. Bake at 375. F for 25 min.

United Church Women - Fogo Island

SNOWBALL DESSERT

1 1/2 tbsp. gelatine	4 tbsp. cold water	1 cup boiling water	1 pkg. Dream Whip
dash of salt	1 cup sugar	1 cup orange juice	1 cake mix (white)
1 cup shredded cocoanut	1 pint whipped cream or	1 tin of cream	juice of 1 lemon or 1 1/4 cups lemon juice

Add gelatine to cold water. Stir in boiling water until the gelatine is dissolved. Add salt, sugar, orange juice & lemon juice. Let mixture partially set. Fold in whipped cream. Line a deep bowl with waxed paper. Prepare cake mix as per instructions and cut all brown surface from edges when finished. Then break the cake in 1" pieces. Put alternate layers of gelatine mixture and cake pieces into the bowl, making sure that the last one is a gelatine layer. Refrigerate over night. Turn out on a plate and frost with Dream Whip and shredded cocoanut.

Mrs. William Anthony - Seldom Come By

APPLE CRUMBLE

1 egg	2 tbsp. flour	1/8 tsp. salt	2/3 cup sugar
ice cream or custard sauce.	1/2 tsp. vanilla	1 tsp. baking powder	1/4 cup walnuts
1/2 tsp. almond extract	1 cup coarsely grated peeled apples		

Heat oven to 350 F. Grease an 8" round layer cake pan. Beat egg and sugar together. Stir in flour, baking powder, salt, vanilla and almond extract. Fold in nuts and apples. Spoon into prepared pan and spread evenly. Bake 35 minutes. Spoon into individual serving dishes or sherbert glasses while warm and serve topped with ice cream or custard sauce. (serves 4 to 6).

Mrs. Claude Gill - Fogo

Water Boy" in
August month.

Water boy keeps busy in AUGUST month bringing his turns of water from the well to the house. Young and old alike share in his homely chore using wagons, hoops, frames and poles to bear the weight of the laden pails.

FROSTY FRUIT PIE

Filling: Bring to a boil 1 1/4 cups crushed pineapple. Stir in 1 pkg. lemon flavoured gelatine. Mix in 3/4 to 1 cup sugar. Cool until almost stiff. Mix until stiff 1 cup undiluted carnation milk. Add 1 tbsp. lemon juice & continue to whip until it forms stiff peaks. Pour on top of the gelatine mixture. Beat in slowly with rotary beater. Pour into baked pie shell. Chill 1 hour.

Success tip: Chill milk until soft ice crystals form around edges - 15 to 20 minutes before whipping. For a fluffy high pie be sure the gelatine mixture is almost stiff, and milk whipped in stiff peaks.

Mrs. Stella Decker - Joe Batt's Arm

GRAHAM WAFER PIE

1 1/2 cups graham wafers rolled fine   1/4 cup melted butter   1/4 cup sugar

   Mix above ingredients thoroughly & put aside 1/4 cup crumbs for top.

2 cups milk   2 1/2 tsp. cornstarch   3 egg yolks   pinch of salt   5 tsp. sugar

   Mix the milk, egg yolks, sugar and cornstarch and cook in double boiler until mixture thickens, stirring constantly to keep free from lumps. Pour over crust.

   Mix 3 egg whites & beat until very stiff, adding gradually 3 tbsp. sugar. Spread over top of pie & finally sprinkle with remainder graham mixture and bake until light brown.

Publisher's note: Above recipe was always a favourite to visiting ministers.

Mrs. Manuel Reid - Barr'd Islands

LEMON SPONGE

1 cup sugar	1 pinch salt	1 cup milk	1 tbsp. butter
2 eggs	3 tbsp. flour	juice of 1 lemon	

Cream butter & sugar. Add flour & salt. Separate eggs. Beat yolks into creamed mixture. Add lemon juice and mix well. Add milk. Beat egg whites stiff and fold in last. Pour into greased casserole and bake in moderate oven 350 F. for 30 - 35 minutes.

LEMON SPONGE PIE

1 pastry shell	1cup sugar	2 eggs separated	1/4 tsp. salt
1/2 cup butter	1 tbsp. lemon rind	1/2 tsp. baking powder	1/4 cup lemon juice
2 tbsp. flour	1 cup milk		

Preheat oven to 450 F. Line pie plate inside with rolled out pastry. Trim and crimp border. Beat egg whites until stiff. Blend sugar, butter, egg yolks and lemon rind and mx in lemon juice. Measure your flour, baking powder and salt into a small sieve and sprinkle over the sugar mixture. Combine lightly then gradually stir in milk. Fold in beaten egg whites. Pour mixture into unbaked pie shell. Bake 10 minutes then lower temperature. Continue to bake pie until filling is set and pastry cooked about 25 minutes longer. Serve warm. Serves 6.

Florence Flight, Sunnyside

LEMON BREAD

1/3 cup margarine	1 1/2 cups flour	1/2 cup milk	1 cup sugar
1 tsp. baking powder	juice & rind of 1 lemon	2 eggs	1/2 tsp. salt

Cream butter & sugar, beating a lot. Add eggs & beat well after each addition. Sift flour, baking powder & salt, and add to butter mixture. Add milk & lemon rind. Bake in loaf pan 1 hour at 350 F, Remove from oven and while still hot pour over bread the juice of 1 lemon which has been combined with 1/4 cup sugar. Let cool and remove from pan.

Mrs. Eunice Budgell, Lewisporte, Nfld.

BRIDE'S PASTRY

1/2 lb. shortening	1/4 cup butter	3 cups sifted flour	1 tsp. salt
1/2 cup cold water			

Cream shortening & butter thoroughly. Add sifted flour & salt gradually, creaming well after each addition. Add water to mixture. Mixture will be sticky at first, so stir well. Use plenty of flour when rolling out. This pastry will never be tough and will keep in refrigerator for 10 days. Sure success recipe for every Bride.

Mrs. Betty Kinden, Stag Harbour

RAISIN PIE FILLING

1 lb. raisins	2 tbsp. corn starch	1/2 cup sugar	1 tsp. salt
1 tbsp. lemon juice			

Place raisins in saucepan & barely cover with cold water. Bring to a boil and cook for 10 minutes. Combine sugar, salt & corn starch. and mix well. Add a little boiling water from the raisins and mix. Stir into remaining boiling water and raisin mixture in saucepan.

Cook over high heat, stirring constantly until thick and clear, about five minutes. Remove from heat and stir in lemon juice. Cool before using.

Makes enough filling for one 9" pie.

Mrs. Thelma Freake · Joe Batt' s Arm

FINE PUFF PASTRY

One lb. flour, a little more for rolling pin and board, and 1/2 lb. butter and 1/2 lb. lard. Cut the butter and lard through the flour (which should be sifted) into small thin shells and mix with sufficient ice water to roll easily. Avoid kneading it and use the hands as little as possible in mixing.

"This method is well over 100 years old."

United Church Women · Fogo Island.

POTATO PORK CAKES (NORTHERN STYLE)

Boil & mash about 8 large potatoes. Cut up finely 1 lb. salt pork (fat back) and fry out until crisp. Drain off fat and add the crisp pork to the mashed potato.

Next sift 3 tsp. baking powder into 2 1/2 cups sifted flour. Add to potato mixture. Form into buns and bake at 350 F. until brown & crusty, about 1/2 hour.

"When the writer lived in the North, the men went out on the ice to hunt seals. Sometimes they would be carried off on the ice and perhaps be off all night. One could see at night the reflection of light from where they were burning seal oil to keep themselves warm. Next morning when the wind changed and the ice returned, wives went off to meet their husbands with bottles of hot tea and hot pork cakes. They would give the men a rest by taking their tow of seals and hauling them for a while"

Florence Wilkinson - Moores Topsail

FAT PORK CAKE

1 lb. fat pork	1/2 lb. citron	4 cups flour	2 tsp. cinnamon
1 lb. raisins	1/2 cup nuts	2 tsp. cloves	2 tsp. baking soda
1 lb. currants	2 cups sugar	2 tsp. spice	1 cup boiling water

Cut up fat pork & pour boiling water over it and mix well. Drain. Add sugar and other ingredients. Dissolve baking soda in boiling water and add to dry ingredients. Mix well. Bake 325 F. oven for 2 to 2 1/2 hours.

"This recipe was my Grandmother's and she would make this cake every week to feed us hungry grandchildren."

Mrs. Helen Sheppard, Carbonear, South, Nfld.

MOLASSES BUNS - 1 cup molasses; 1/2 cup butter; 1/2 tsp. vanilla; 1 cup raisins; 3 cups flour; 1 tsp. soda; 1 1/2 spoon baking powder; 1 tsp. nutmeg & 1 tsp. cinnamon. Mix together all ingredients & bake until done.

"I have been baking these buns for 20 years or more."

Mrs. Charles Brinston, North Hr. P. B.

OLD FASHIONED DARK CAKE

1 cup molasses	3 eggs	1/4 cup milk	1 tsp. coffee
3 cups flour	3/4 cup salt pork fat	1 tsp. vanilla	1 tsp. baking soda
1/2 lb. raisins	1/2 tsp. each of spice, cinnamon and cloves		

Combine flour, spices & raisins. Mix molasses, port fat & eggs well beaten. Add coffee in two tsp. water to vanilla & milk. Dissolve baking soda in hot water and add all liquid mixtures to dry ingredients. Bake 2 hours at 300 F.

"This recipe was used by my grandmother who died in 1912 at the age of 82; ie; born 1830. It has been used by members of her family through the years and no doubt was also used by my great grandmother before."
Iola M. Winsor, Newtown, B. Bay.

OLD FASHIONED GINGERBREAD CAKE

2 cans tomato soup	1 cup raisins	3 eggs beaten
1 cup walnuts (chopped)	2 pkgs. gingerbread mix	

Mix soup & eggs in large bowl. Sift the gingerbread. Mix & beat with beater at low speed for 2 minutes. Fold in raisins and chopped nuts. Pour into 9" tube pan greased. Bake at 325 F. for 1 hour. Cool right side up in pan for 10 minutes. Serve warm or cold.
Mrs. Alfreda Parson, Garden Cove.

OLD NEWFOUNDLAND CUSTOM: "The old custom is that Christmas Celebration begins on Christmas Eve with a Thanksgiving meal of salt fish followed by sweet raisin bread called 'Christmas Fruit Loaf.' Fishing was the means of livelihood and so fish had its place in thanksgiving before the day of feasting."
United Church Women, Swift Current

OLD TIME PORK MOLASSES CAKE

1 cup salt pork (cut fine)	1 tsp. baking soda	2/3 cup molasses	1 cup currants
1 cup strong coffee	2 eggs, well beaten	3 cups sifted flour	1 cup mixed peel
1 cup sugar	1 tsp. spice	2 cups raisins	

Place pork in a bowl, pour hot coffee over it. Let cool. Combine sugar, spices, soda. Stir into pork mixture, then add eggs & molasses. Sprinkle 2 tablespoons flour over fruit. Add rest of flour to the pork mixture, then add floured fruit. Bake at 275 F. for about 3 hours.

Mrs. Greta Beazley, Garden Cove & Mrs. Mae Moulton, Burin Bay Arm

PORK CAKES

1 cup minced salt pork	2 tsp. baking powder	6 potatoes	1 tsp. baking soda
2 cups flour			

Cook potatoes & mash well. Add pork & mix well with potatoes. Add flour, baking powder and soda. Mix together with hands and form into cakes. Bake at 400 F. for 1/2 to 1 hour or until brown.

"These cakes are traditional in my home town (Grand Bank) and are usually made every Satur-day."

Mrs. Allan Arbeau, St. Georges

TEA BUNS

4 cups flour	1 cup raisins	1 tsp. vanilla	1/2 lb. butter
4 tsp. baking powder	1 cup sugar	1 egg	

Place flour in mixing bowl. Rub butter through flour. Put all other ingredients in the flour & mix the milk & water to a soft batter. Roll and cut out with cutter.

"This recipe was given to me around 50 years ago from my aunt. It's a delicious tea bun."

Mrs. Winnie Piercey, Garden Cove, P. B.

BLUEBERRY CAKE

1 cup sugar	1 1/2 cups flour	2 eggs	few grains salt
1/3 cup butter	1/2 cup milk	1 tsp. lemon flavouring	1 cup blueberries
2 tsp. baking powder			

Cream butter thoroughly and add the sugar gradually. Cream together well. Add well beaten eggs. Sift flour 3 times, baking powder & salt. Add flour alternately with milk. Add flavouring. Add berries and mix lightly. Pour into a greased loaf pan & bake in a moderate over about 45 minutes.

Thelma Freake - Joe Batt's Arm.

ORANGE DATE CAKE

1 cup boiling water	1 tbsp. grated orange rind	3 eggs separated	2 tsp. soda
1 cup finely chopped dates	1 1/2 cups sugar	2 cups flour	1/4 cup orange juice
3/4 cup shortening			

Pour boiling water over dates & orange rind in bowl. LET STAND. Cream sugar, shortening & egg yolk thoroughly. Measure flour (without sifting), baking powder, soda & salt onto square waxed paper. Stir well to blend. Add dry ingredients alternately with combined orange juice and water to creamed mixture. Stir date mixture and blend into batter. Beat egg whites until stiff and fold into batter. Spread in greased and lightly floured 9" X 13" pan.

Bake at 350 F. for 50 to 55 minutes. Cool in pan. Frost with orange butter icing or as desired.

Mrs. Stanley Pope - Fogo

WILLS AND WIVES: Men dying, make their wills - but wives
        escape a work so sad;
    Why should they make what all their lives
        the gentle dames have had?

Submitted by Mrs. Florence Wilkinson-Moores

WALNUT CAKE

1 cup sugar	1/2 cup shortening	1 cup flour	1 tsp. salt
1 tbsp. cinnamon	1 tsp. baking powder	3/4 cup chopped walnuts	1/2 cup milk
2 eggs, beaten separately			

Cream shortening & sugar. Add egg yolks beaten with milk. Sift flour, baking powder and cinnamon. Mix with walnuts and add to first mixture. Fold in whites of eggs beaten stiff. Bake in moderate oven. Cover with any desired frosting.

"This recipe is over one hundred years old."

Mrs. Ralph Giles, Garden Cove

BANANA CAKE

1/2 cup butter	1 cup sugar	2 eggs, beaten	1 tsp. vanilla
1 tsp. baking soda	4 tsp. boiling water	1 cup mashed bananas	1/2 tsp. salt
2 cups sifted pastry flour	1 tsp. baking powder	1 cup chopped nuts	

Cream butter & sugar, add beaten eggs. Dissolve soda in boiling water and add mashed bananas. Sift flour, baking powder and salt. Add alternately with banana mixture, adding nuts and vanilla last. Bake at 350 F. for 40 minutes in a greased 8" square pan.

"This recipe is a Canadian recipe and over a hundred years old. It is a treasured family favourite and a selected prize recipe."

Mrs. George Eddy, Garden Cove, Plac. Bay.

DARK CAKE

3/4 cup butter	1 cup sugar	1 cup dates	1 cup molasses
2 cups raisins	2 cups currants	3 eggs	4 tsp. baking powder
1 tsp. soda	spice of all kinds	1/2 cup mixed peel	flour to stiffen

Mrs. Oswald Dominix, Little Bay East, F. Bay.

CAKE MADE IN A HURRY

3 cups flour	1 tsp. baking powder	2 tbsp. melted butter	1 tsp. salt
1 egg	1 cup milk or water	1 cup white sugar	2 tsp. Cream Tartar

Put all dry ingredients into a bowl and mix well. Make hole in centre, drop in egg, melted butter and milk. Beat all together till light. Bake in greased cake pan for 30 to 40 minutes.

United Church Women - Seldom Come By

MIRACLE CAKE

1/3 cup butter	2 cups sifted flour	1 tsp. baking powder	1/4 tsp. salt
1 tsp. nutmeg	1 cup sugar	1 tsp. cinnamon	1 tsp. allspice
10 oz. can tomato soup	1 cup chopped nuts	1 tsp. baking soda	2 egg yolks
1 cup chopped raisins			

Cream butter; add sugar gradually. Beat until light & fluffy. Beat egg yolks with electric beater until thick & a pale lemon colour. Add fat-sugar mixture, beating thoroughly until creamy. Mix flour with salt, baking soda, baking powder & spices. Sift together 4 or 5 times.

Add dry ingredients alternately with soup (adding about 1/4 at a time) beginning and ending with dry ingredients. Stir gently & quickly until batter is well blended together. Do not over mix. Fold in nuts and raisins. Spread carefully in a greased 9 inch square pan and bake in moderate oven at 350 F. for 55 to 60 minutes.

Mrs. Wesley L. Sheppard - Stag Harbour

LONELY HEARTS? TRY FASTING!

A woman who fasted for sixty-two days
To see if the stunt could be done;
From hundreds of Scotsmen had letters of praise,
And proposals from seventy-one.

Submitted by Mrs. Florence Wilkinson-Moores

Berry Picking

Lorie Jespersor

Come **SEPTEMBER month** the excitement of berry picking brings many Newfoundland families out to the marshes and hills. Bakeapples, partridgeberries, blueberries, squashberries, black berries, raspberries, marsh berries, wild cherries, gooseberries, red and black currants and sarsparilla await the joyful families bearing flour sacks, pots, pans and pails to harvest the crop. Nor is the occasion complete without the traditional 'boil up' which marks a fitting climax to a day under open skies.

SPONGE CAKE

4 eggs well beaten   1 1/2 tsp. baking powder   1 cup white sugar   1 tsp. allspice
1/2 cup hot milk, not real hot

Beat eggs good, then put in sugar gradually and beat well. Then add the flour which has been sifted three times with baking powder. I always beat it in with a large spoon. Last, the hot milk is added. I folds it in with spoon. Bake for 20 minutes.

"It is really a good sponge cake. I put it together with Dream Whip. If you know Mrs. Kewley, she can tell you it's a good Sponge Cake."

Mrs. Gladys Garland, Lower Island Cove, C.B., Nfld.

BOILED DARK CAKE

1/2 cup butter   1/2 lb. dates   1 tsp cinnamon   1/2 tsp. salt
2 cups hot water   1 lb. raisins   1 tsp. mace   1 tsp. cloves
2 cups brown sugar

Boil together for 5 minutes, let cool. Add the following:

2 beaten eggs   1/2 cup nuts   1 tsp. almond flavouring   4 oz. cherries
3 cups flour   1/2 cup mixed peel   1 tsp baking powder

Bake 1 1/2 hours at 325 F.

Mrs. Eunice Eudgell, Lewisporte, Nfld.

VINEGAR PIE

| 1 cup vinegar | 1/2 tsp. cream | 1 1/2 cups water | 1/2 tsp. spice | 1/2 cup sugar |

Boil above ingredients together for 10 minutes then thicken with corn starch. Then make any ordinary pastry and put filling in pie.

"This recipe was used by my mother many years ago. She grew her own vinegar plants. One half gallon of molasses water sweetened to taste and a small piece of vinegar plant placed in the container will keep the plant growing until the container is full and you always have Vinegar to use when you need it."   *Mrs. Frank Boyd, Summerford, Nfld.*

BOILED DARK FRUIT CAKE

1 lb. raisins	1 lb. currants	1/2 lb. dates	1/2 lb. cherries
1/2 cup walnuts	1/2 cup mixed fruit	2 cups water	2 cups brown sugar
1 cup butter	1 tsp. cinnamon	1 tsp. cloves	1 tsp. allspice
1 tsp. vanilla			

Prepare & cut up fruit & add all ingredients and put in large pot. Simmer on top of stove for 15 minutes. Let cool a little then add 3 cups flour & 2 tsp. baking soda and mix well. Bake 2 1/2 to 3 hours.

"This cake recipe can be used for any occasion. I personally have been making this cake for a long time and have had no failures. It can be stored in containers and the longer it is stored, the more moistened it becomes. For a larger cake the recipe can be doubled. I found this recipe quite a long time ago from a dietician's book and passed it on to my sisters, relatives and many friends. They have had good results from it as well."   *Mrs. Florence Bursey, New Melbourne, T. Bay.*

NEWFOUNDLAND SAYING: "Fair weather to you and snow to your heels."- means good luck on your way.   *Mrs. Pearl Hatfield, Collins Cove, Burin*

DARK FRUIT CAKE

1 lb. brown sugar	1 lb. raisins	1 pkg. cherries	1/2 tsp. salt
3 1/2 cups flour	1 tbsp. mace	3/4 cup milk	1 pkg. dates
1/2 lb. butter	1 lb. currants	1 pkg. mixed peel	3 eggs
1 tsp. allspice	1/2 tsp. soda	1/4 lb. walnuts	1 tsp. cinnamon

1 tsp. vanilla - or whatever flavouring preferred

Cream butter and sugar. Add one egg at a time. Beat thoroughly until fluffy. The more you beat it, the finer the cake will be. Sift flour and then measure. Take some of the flour and dredge your fruit before the spices are added. To the remaining flour add the spices, salt and soda. Sift 3 times and add to creamed mixture alternately with milk. Add nuts, vanilla and dredged fruit. Bake 3 to 3 1/2 hours in moderate oven (350 F). If preferred, you can add a drop of spirits of any kind which will help keep the cake moist for a long time.

Mrs. Brendon McKenna, Island Harbour

MOLASSES CAKE

One cup butter, 1 cup brown sugar, 1 cup molasses, 1 cup sweet milk, 3 cups flour, four eggs, 1 1/2 tsp. cream tartar, one tsp. soda, 2 lb. raisins chopped fine and nutmeg. Bake in slow oven.

"This recipe over 100 years old."

United Church Women - Fogo Island

THE CAUSE OF ALL THE TROUBLE?

God made the world, and rested.
God made man - and rested.
Then God made women;
Since then, neither God nor man has rested.

Submitted by Mrs. Florence Wilkinson-Moores

TOMATO SOUP CAKE

1/3 cup butter	1 tsp. baking soda	1 tsp. cinnamon	1/2 cup peel
1 cup brown sugar	1 1/2 cups flour	1 cup raisins	1 tsp. cloves
1 can tomato soup	1 tsp. baking powder		

Cream butter and sugar. Dissolve soda in soup and beat into the butter and sugar mix. Sift flour, baking powder and spices twice, and add to first mixture. Stir in floured raisins and peel. Turn into greased pan and bake 350 F for 50 min.

United Church Women - Fogo Island

BOILED FRUIT CAKE

1 pkg. raisins	cherries	2 cups white sugar	2 tsp. cloves
1 pkg. currants	few nuts	1 tsp. spice	2 tbsp. Cocoa
mixed peel	1 lb. butter	1 tsp. cinnamon	2 cups cold water

Mix all together in pot to boil 10 to 15 minutes. Stir in 2 teaspoons baking soda and 2 cups boiling water and flavouring. Put back to cool, then add 5 cups flour. Bake 3 hours in slow over.

United Church Women - Fogo Island

LIGHT FRUIT CAKE

1/2 lb. butter	1 cup warm milk	2 1/2 cups cake flour	4 eggs
2 cups white sugar	1 tsp. vanilla	3/4 cup plain flour	1/2 lb. fruit
1 tsp. baking powder	1/2 lb. fruit	3/4 cup corn flour	

Cream together butter and sugar well by hand. Then add eggs one at a time and beat again. Add half of flour all kinds sifted together with baking powder. Beat again. Add rest of flour and vanilla. Let stand for 5 minutes. Add fruit, beat again. Bake 1 1/2 hours.

Stella Green - Fogo

WHITE LINIMENT — For Muscular Pains, etc.

"When I was a bedlamer boy seventy-five years ago, medical aid in outport communities was sort of confined to the skills of local elderly ladies. Although they did not have any formal medical training, they were skilled in the old time use of herbs and other ingredients when administering to the sick and ailing residents living in the communities where those skilled ladies resided.

One Sunday afternoon as I sat relaxing in my cozy corner where I do my planning and writing, my wife sitting in her rocker nearby said, "Why not write a recipe for old time white liniment used extensively three quarters of a century ago."

Old time medicine men when advertising their bottled products stated the concoction as a cure-all for all ailments.

The liniment I am referring to long years ago was proven to be effective when used externally for rheumatic pains, sprains, neuralgia, neuritis, leg cramp and other muscular ailments. When 1 was a young lad eight years old I can well remember my Grandfather George Hann describing to my mother the ingredients and methods for making this liniment. He had received the information from some old lady of his acquaintance.

In the bygone days, or as some old people referred to times passed, as "pot-augus-days', egg cups were extensively used as measuring cups."

Recipe: Take two egg cups full white vinegar; two egg cups full spirits turpentine and the whites of two eggs with shells.

Place the above ingredients in bottle. Shake bottle occasionally until egg shells dissolved.

"I am well aware of the use of this liniment for many years. It was an excellent relief when used to rub painful affected areas and compared favorably with other liniments then on the market."

Submitted to F. B. & M. by Victor, Arnold's Cove, P. Bay, Nfld.

GRANDMA' S FAVOURITE DARK CAKE

4 cups flour	1/2 lb. peel	1 cup boiling water	1 cup molasses
1 pkg. currants	2 tsp. soda	1 pkg. raisins	1 cup white sugar
1 lb. fat back pork	1 tsp. each nutmeg, mace & cloves		

Mince pork & pour boiling water over it. Add molasses & sugar and beat well. Sift flour & soda. Add spices & fruit and mix well. Bake 2 1/2 to 3 hours in slow oven.

Mrs. G. Hart, Fogo, Notre Dame Bay, Nfld

FRUIT CAKE

1 cup sugar	2 cups sifted flour	1 cup white raisins	1 1/2 cups water
1/2 cup mixed fruit	1 tsp. baking powder	1 tsp. soda	1/3 cup shortening
1/2 cup chopped nuts			

Combine sugar, water, shortening & raisins and bring to boil for 2 minutes. Cool. Add combined flour, baking powder, soda, salt, fruit and nuts. Mix well and pour into baking tin and bake 1 hour or until done. Hint: When baking cakes, place a saucepan of warm water near cake. This helps to keep cake soft & moist.

Mrs. Cyril Mahaney, Fogo, Nfld.

TEA BUNS

3 cups flour	salt	1 egg slightly beaten	3 tsp. baking powder
1/2 cup butter	1 cup water (approx)	1/3 cup sugar	1 tsp. lard

Sift dry ingredients & cut or rub in butter. Mix with egg & water. Do not over mix. Roll out & cut buns. Bake in hot oven at 450 F. for approx. 20 minutes.

Mrs. Madeline Leyte, Fogo, Nfld.

MRS. SMALLWOOD' S FRUIT CAKE

1 lb. raisins or currants	1 lb. dates	1/4 lb. mixed peel	2 tsp. almond flavouring
2 tsp. lemon flavouring	1/2 cup warm water	1 cup chopped nuts	1/2 cup brown sugar
3 eggs	1 cup cherries	2 1/2 cups flour	1 tsp. soda
2 tsp. maple flavouring	1 lb. butter	1 tsp. vanilla	1 tsp. spices

Cream butter and sugar. Add eggs and cream well. Add flavouring. Sift flour and spices together then coat fruit with 1 cup flour and spice mixture. Add the fruit to butter mixture and then remainder of flour. Add the soda dissolved in 1/2 cup of warm water and then if desired, add one cup of strawberry jam. Bake in 275 F. for 3 1/2 hours. (note: when storing, wrap in wet "J" cloths or foil wrap).

"This cake is used around Christmas time. The earlier it is made the nicer the flavour. I first found this recipe in a 'Weekend Telegram.' Mrs. Smallwood, the wife of Mr. J. R. Smallwood, that is, Newfoundland' s first Premier after Newfoundland joined Confederation in 1949, submitted the recipe to the paper."

Dora Eddy, North Harbour

COCOA CAKE

1/2 cup cocoa	1 cup milk	1 egg	1 tsp. baking powder
1 tsp. soda	1 1/2 cups flour	1 cup white sugar	1/2 tsp. salt
1 tsp. vanilla	2 tbsp. butter		

Blend cocoa with 1 1/2 cups milk & cook until thick. Remove from heat and beat in egg yolk. Cream butter and sugar & add remaining 1/2 cup milk. Sift flour with baking powder, soda and salt. Add to mixture. Lastly, add the beaten egg whites.

Mrs. Hedley Butler, Burin

BIRTHDAY CAKE

1 lb. prunes (cut up & soften in a drop of water)	1 cup small figs	1 tsp. cloves,citron,peel	2 cups sugar
	1 cup butter	1 cup molasses	5 to 7 eggs
1 1/2 tsp. cinnamon	2 cups currants	1 cup walnuts	1 1/2 tsp. spice
5 tsp. baking powder	flour enough to make stiff batter (5 cups)		

Bake in an iron pot in 275 F. oven for 3 1/2 hours.

Mrs. Parmenas Wells - Fogo

MOLASSES TAFFY

2 cups molasses	2 tbsp. butter	1 cup sugar	1 tbsp. vinegar

Place all ingredients in a saucepan. Boil until mixture becomes brittle - hard crack stage (when a drop put in cold water forms a ball), pour into buttered pan. Grease hands and when cool enough to handle, pull the toffee until it becomes light in colour. Cut into pieces with scissors.

Mrs. R.E. Holmes - Seldom Come By

CRY BABIES (Molasses Cookies)

1 cup hot coffee	1 cup white sugar	1 tblsp. ginger	1 tblsp. vinegar
1 cup molasses	2 eggs	1 tsp. cinnamon	little salt
1 cup shortening	4 1/2 cups flour	2 tsp. soda	

Mix coffee, molasses, shortening, sugar and eggs. Put little hot water in baking soda and add to mixture. Add dry ingredients, with more flour if necessary. Add vinegar last. Drop by spoonful on baking sheet and bake in moderate oven.

Mrs. Eunice Budgell, Lewisporte, Nfld.

PEACH FRUIT CAKE

1 cup butter	1 tin peaches	1 1/2 cups coconut	1/2 tsp. salt
1 1/2 cups sugar	1 1/2 cups raisins	3 cups flour	2 tsp. vanilla
3 eggs well beaten	1 1/2 cups cherries	1 tsp. baking powder	

Cream butter, sugar. Add eggs. Add dry ingredients. Blend crushed and drained peaches. Add raisins, cherries, vanilla and coconut. Juice may be added if the batter is too dry. Bake at 270 F. for 3 hours.

United Church Women, Fogo Island.

DESSERT - SPANISH CREAM

To 4 cups of milk add 2 pkgs. gelatine previously soaked in 1/4 cup cold milk. Add 1 cup sugar to beaten egg yolks of four eggs and pour into boiling milk. Let it boil for a moment. Add flavouring. Have four whites beaten stiff and fold the mixture into whites. Stir around.

Nellie Coish - Stag Harbour

PEACH CAKE

1 cup butter	1 tin (15oz) sliced peaches	1 pkg. red cherries	1 pkg. green cherries
3 cups raisins	3 eggs	1 tsp. vanilla	1 tsp. baking powder
1 1/4 cups sugar	1 cup coconut	3 cups flour	

Cream butter & sugar. Add unbeaten eggs, beating well after each addition. Sift flour & baking powder together and add to the creamed mixture. Then add all fruit. Bake in oven at 275 F.

Dorothy E. Collins - Stag Harbour

Having a 'Cuffer' at the Harvest Supper

OCTOBER is the month for the Harvest Supper, an occasion which brings out the whole community. Nine or ten women will 'take a table' each, adorning it with white cloth, cutlery, utensils and such delicacies that will make mouths water and hungry stomachs growl. After eating, friends will gather to have a 'cuffer' about the events of the day. Not unnoticable are the children who run and play, awaiting their turn to eat. Without a doubt, the Harvest Supper was one of the prime inspirations for "Fat-Back and Molasses", for most of the foods which blessed the tables will be found in this book.

BUTTERSCOTCH FINGERS

Batter:
1 cup sifted all-purpose flour
1 cup shortening
1/2 tsp. salt
1 tbsp. cold water

Mixture:
2 eggs well beaten   1 tsp. vanilla   1/2 tsp. salt
1 cup brown   1/2 tsp. sugar   1/4 tsp. baking powder
1/2 cup nuts chopped   2 tbsp. sifted all-purpose flour
1/4 cp. marashino cherries chopped

Sift together 1 cup flour and the salt and cut in the shortening until the mixture is crumbly. Add the cold water and blend. This dough is very stiff. Press the batter into an oiled pan 8 inches by 12. Bake in a hot oven (400 F.) for 12 - 15 minutes.

Remove from the oven and spread the following mixture over the partly cooked base. Beat the eggs till very light. Add brown sugar, beat again until the sugar is dissolved. Add chopped nuts, cherries, vanilla, 2 tbsp. flour, salt and baking powder. Blend lightly. Spread this mixture over the partly cooked batter. Bake in a moderate oven for 35 minutes. Cut in finger lengths while still warm.

Gladys Garland, Lower Island Cove, C.B., Nfld

LEMON SQUARES

Rub together:
1/4 lb. butter   10 sodas rolled fine   1 cup flour   pinch salt
1 tsp. baking powder   1 cup coconut   1 scant cup sugar

Mix and cook in double boiler. When boiling hot, add 2 tbsp. corn flour mixed with half cup cold water. Cook till thick.

Filling:
1 cup sugar   2 eggs   1 cup cold water   Juice and rind of 1 lemon   2 tsp. butter

Spread half the thickened flour mixture in bottom of pan 7 inches by 11. Cover with hot lemon filling. Spread remaining mixture on top. Sprinkle with coconut. Bake in moderate oven till brown.

Mrs. Gladys Garland, Lower Island Cove, C.B., Nfld.

PINEAPPLE UPSIDE DOWN CAKE

3 tbsp. margarine	maraschino cherries	1 1/2 tsp. baking powder	1 tsp. vanilla
1 1/4 cups sifted cake flour	1 can sliced pineapple	1/3 cup brown sugar	1/2 tsp. salt
1/2 cup granulated sugar	1/3 cup shortening	1 egg	

Topping: Melt margarine in 9" X 1 1/2" round baking dish. Drain pineapple, reserving 1/2 cup syrup. Arrange cherries in bottom of dish. Cover with brown sugar then pineapple.

Cake: Cream together shortening and granulated sugar. Add egg and vanilla, then beat till fluffy. Sift together dry ingredients. Add alternately with reserved pineapple syrup, beating after each addition. Spread over pineapple. Bake in moderate over (350 F. for 45 to 50 minutes). Let stand 5 minutes and invert on plate. Serve warm.

Stella Decker - Joe Batt's Arm

BULL' S EYES

1 cup brown sugar	1 cup molasses	2 tbsp. lemon juice	2 tbsp. butter

Cook all together in sauce pan. Do not stir while cooking until you test a few drops in cold water. When it forms a ball pour all out on greased platter until it cools sufficiently to handle.

Grease hands and pull and manipulate until it is a lovely golden brown and snappy to touch. Pull and roll in long narrow strings about the size of a thumb. Cut into one inch pieces with scissors and arrange on greased platter to set hard.

"Bull's Eyes were always made for the Christmas season and they always provided lots of fun when young people got together for a "taffy-pull."

Florence Wilkinson-Moores, Topsail

CUFFER - "A meeting of fishermen or seamen, generally aboard a ship, to have a friendly chat or to swap yarns."

E. R. Hann, Wesleyville, B. B., Nfld.

RAISIN - APPLE COFFEE CAKE

2 cups sifted flour	1 cup sugar	3 tsp. baking powder	1 tsp. salt
1/3 cup soft butter	1 egg	1 cup milk	1/2 cup raisins
1 cup finely grated peeled apples		1/2 cup sugar	1 1/2 tsp. cinnamon

Heat oven 350 F. Grease 9" square cake pan. Sift flour, 1 cup sugar, baking powder & salt together into mixing bowl. Add butter. Beat egg and milk together lightly with a fork and add to flour mixture. Beat hard for 2 minutes. Stir in apples and raisins. Spoon into prepared pan. Spread evenly. Combine 1/2 cup sugar and cinnamon and sprinkle over top of batter.

Bake about 35 minutes or until a toothpick stuck in centre comes out clean. Serve warm.

Mrs. Shirley Temple, Sunnyside, Nfld.

PARTRIDGEBERRY SQUARES

3 tbsp. butter	2 egg yolks	1/4 tsp. salt	2/3 cup flour
1/4 tsp. vanilla	1/4 cup milk	1/3 cup sugar	1 tsp. baking powder

Cream butter, sugar and egg yolks. Add dry ingredients with milk and vanilla. Bake in 8" square pan about 18 minutes at 350 F.

Topping for above squares:

3 egg whites	6 tbsp. sugar	dash salt	1 cup partridgeberries

Beat egg whites stiff with salt. Add sugar, beat again, fold in berries. Return to oven, Bake for 12 minutes.

Sybil Blake, North West River, Labrador

PINEAPPLE FRUIT CAKE

6 cups coconut	1/2 lb. blanched almonds	3 eggs	2 tsp. baking powder
3/4 cup soft butter	1 tsp. almond extract	1 tsp. salt	1 lb. raisins
1 tsp. vanilla	1 cup sugar	3 cups sifted flour	
1 - 10 oz. can crushed pineapple, pulp and juice		1/2 lb. candied cherries,	

Mix coconut, cherries, raisins and almonds in large bowl. Cream butter in another bowl. Add sugar gradually, beating well. Add eggs and beat until light and very fluffy. Stir in pineapple and flavourings. Sift flour, baking powder and salt together over fruit. Mix with hands until all fruit is coated. Add to creamed mixture and stir until blended.

Line a 10 inch tube pan with greased wax paper. Heat oven to 300 F. and bake 1 3/4 hours to 2 hours.

Flora Primmer - Barr'd Islands

PINEAPPLE CAKE

1 cup white sugar	3 cups flour	1 cup butter	1/2 tsp. salt
1 lb. raisins	1/2 lb. peel	2 eggs	2 tsp. baking powder
1 lb. cherries	1 tin crushed pineapple (drained)		

Mix ingredients and bake 2 1/2 hours in oven at 300 to 350 F. *Mrs Sarah Brown - Joe Batt's Arm*

HONEY TARTS

2 eggs, beaten	2 cups brown sugar	1/4 tsp. nutmeg	1 cup water	1 tbsp. honey

Boil sugar & water to a light syrup. Cool. Add eggs, honey, nutmeg and beat thoroughly. Fill unbaked tart shells. Bake at 450 F. for 10 minutes. Reduce heat to 350 F. for 15 minutes.

"Labrador Cook Book"

FAT BACK & LASSY TOUTONS

1 lb. fat pork, chopped fine	2 tsp. baking soda	1 cup sugar
sour milk	1 1/2 cups molasses	3 tsp. each ginger and cinnamon
1 tsp. allspice	5 cups flour	1 1/2 cups hot water

Melt fat pork in oven, let cool. Put flour in large bowl, add sugar and spices. To molasses add baking soda, hot water, and rendered pork and scrunchions, then add this to the flour mixture with enough sour milk to form dough firm enough to roll. Roll on floured board, about 1/2 inch thick and cut. Bake in hot oven for approximately 20 minutes.

"In Brigus, Conception Bay, anywhere from 35 to 100 years ago, the men would leave to go 'in the woods' for firewood at early morning and not return until late afternoon. As this was in zero or sub-zero weather, their lunches would freeze. While they could toast bread and roast fish or caplin over the open fire, they needed something sweet also. My mother and my grandmother before her, always gave the men Fat Bacy and Lassy Toutons, as it was found that these did not freeze."

Hilda Spracklin, St. John's, Nfld.

BOILED PUDDING

1 1/2 cups flour	1 tbsp. each of butter and sugar	1/2 tsp. salt

Enough boiling water to mix a stiff batter. Put in cloth and boil one hour.

"This recipe was passed down by Mrs. Albert Spencer, Springdale, and has been made by our family for seventy years."

Mrs. Mary Grant, Little Bay, Newfoundland

DATE AND NUT BARS

3/4 cup sifted flour	3/4 cup brown sugar	1 cup chopped nuts	1/4 tsp. salt
1 tsp. baking power	2 cups chopped dates	1/4 cup melted butter	3 eggs

Bake in square pan for 45 to 50 minutes. Spread with chocolate frosting and cut in bars.

Mrs. Julia Leyte, Fogo, Nfld.

CORNER BROOK'S MYSTERY ICING

1 cup boiling water   1 tbsp. sugar, added to boiling water
2 rounded tbsp. custard powder mixed with a little cold water

Cook until colour changes. Stir constantly. Let cool, add flavouring (lemon). Meanwhile cream 1/2 lb. butter, add 1/2 cup sugar, small amounts at a time. When this is good and creamy add custard powder mixture by teaspoons and beat well after each addition.

This is an excellent filling as well as an icing for Chocolate cake.

SUSIE'S ICING

4 tbsp. flour   1 cup cold milk   1 cup water   1/2 cup sugar (or 1 cup)   1 tsp. vanilla

Cream butter and vanilla until fluffy. Add sugar gradually and beat until fluffy. Boil flour and milk until thick. Let cool and add the butter and sugar until fluffy. This icing looks like whipped cream.

Mrs. B. Dyke, Nfld.

MY OWN PUDDING

1/4 cup butter   1/2 cup molasses   1/2 cup milk   1 egg
1 1/2 cups flour   1/2 tsp. salt   1/2 tsp. soda
1 cup raisins or blackberries or blueberries

Steam 2 hours.

Mrs. E.A. Babstock, Corner Borrk, Nfld.

DARK CHRISTMAS CAKE

1 cup molasses
5 eggs well beaten
2 cups lemon peel
1 tbsp. vanilla
1 tbsp. cloves
2 cups citron peel
Wine glass whiskey or rum

1 cup butter
2 tsp. salt
1 1/2 cups dates
1 tbsp. cinnamon
3 1/2 cups sifted flour
4 cups mixed peel

1 cup granulated sugar
3 cups raisins
2 tbsp. hot water
1 tbsp. allspice
3 cups currants
1 tsp. soda

Steep spices in molasses over a low heat. Do not let boil. The longer it is allowed to steep the darker your cake will be. Cream butter and sugar, then add well beaten eggs and cooled molasses mixture. Dust fruit with 1/4 cup of the flour, add remainng flour and salt to the butter mixture and blend well. Stir in floured fruit. Last of all, mix in soda dissolved in hot water.

Use a large baking pan lined with three layers of brown paper. An iron pot is best and it should be at least 10 inches deep. Bake at 275 F for 3 to 3 1/2 hours.

"Of course in the old days people cut their own fruit, but now you can use mixed cut peel instead of the lemon and citron if desired. This is my favourite cake. My mother also used this recipe and passed it down to me."

Mrs. B. Dyke, Nfld.

MACE CAKE

Sift together 2 cups flour, 1 cup sugar, 2 tsp. baking powder, 1 tsp. salt, 1 tsp. mace. Add 1/2 cup soft butter and 1 cup milk.

Beat 2 minutes in electric mixer, longer by hand. Add the 2 eggs, beat 2 minutes more. Bake in loaf pan at 350 F. for 30 minutes.

Gladys Garland, Lower Island Cove, C.B., Nfld.

CHRISTMAS CAKE

4 cups flour	2 rounded tbsp. custard powder mixed with a little cold water		
1 lb. sticky raisins	1 tsp. cinnamon	1/4 tsp. cloves	1 pint milk
1 cup butter	1 hp. tsp. baking soda	1/2 lb. currants	1/2 lb.mixed fruit
1/2 tsp. ginger	1 lb. brown sugar		

Rub butter through flour, add sugar & mix well. Add spices & mix well. Add fruit & mix well. Add a little salt. Add milk in which soda has been dissolved. Bake in covered pot for 3 1/2 hours at 275 F. Let cake cool with cover on.

"This recipe is 200 years old and was brought to Newfoundland from Ireland by the Nuns."

Mrs. Eli Foote, Burin, Nfld.

OLD FASHIONED XMAS CAKE

3/4 cup butter	1/2 cup corn syrup	3 eggs	1 cup dates (cut fine)
1/4 tsp. mace	1/4 cup brown sugar	2 cups raisins	3 cups flour
1/2 tsp. cinnamon	3/4 cup molasses	1/2 cup jam	1 cup currants
1/2 tsp. baking soda	1/4 tsp. cloves	1/4 tsp. ginger	1/2 tsp. baking powder
1/2 cup salt pork(cut up fine)			

Cream butter, brown sugar, corn syrup and molasses together. Add eggs. Mix sifted dry ingredients. Add jam and salt pork (wash off salt). Add fruit and mix well. Bake in large iron pot with lid on for about 3 to 4 hours in slow oven.

Mrs. Marie Frost, Hillview

CHRISTMAS CAKE

1 1/2 cups seedless raisins	1 1/2 cups water	1 tsp. baking soda	1 tsp. baking powder
1/4 cup butter	1/2 tsp. cinnamon	1 1/2 cups brown sugar	2 eggs
3 cups flour	1/2 tsp. salt	1/4 tsp. cloves	1/2 tsp. allspice

1 cup of any or all of the following: nuts, dates, candied cherries, mixed peel.

Wash and drain raisins well and mix in a saucepan with water, brown sugar and butter. Bring to a boil and cook gently for 10 minutes. Chill. Dissolve soda in well beaten eggs and add to chilled mixture. Mix and sift flour, baking powder, salt and spices into a bowl and add the cup of mixed nuts and fruit. Stir this dry mixture into liquid mixture and blend well.

Bake in slow oven at 275 F. for 3 hours.

Mrs. Parmenas Wells - Fogo

CHRISTMAS CAKE

1 lb. butter	1 lb. dates	1 lb. peel	1/4 cup rum
1/2 cup brown sugar	1/2 tsp. cloves	1 tsp. allspice	1 tsp. nutmeg
2 1/2 cups flour	1 lb. raisins	1 cup nuts	1/4 cup raspberry jam
3 eggs	1/2 tsp. ginger	1 tsp. mace	1 tsp. cinnamon
2 tsp.vanilla, maple, almond and lemon extract		1 lb. currants	1 cup cherries

1 tsp. soda in 1/4 cup hot water

Cream butter and sugar. Add eggs. Cream well. Add flavourings. Sift flour and spices together. Sprinkle little flour on fruit and nuts. Stir to coat well. Add butter mixture to fruit mixture. Add jam and rum. Bake slowly at 300 F. for 3 hours. (test at 2 1/2 hours)

Mrs. Violet Leyte, Fogo

CHRISTMAS CAKE

2 cups seedless raisins	3/4 tsp. salt	6 eggs	1/3 cup cold strong coffee
1 1/2 tsp. baking powder	1/2 tsp. cloves	2 1/2 cups flour	1 1/2 cups seeded raisins
1 1/2 tsp. nutmeg	1 1/2 cups cherries	1 cup cut up dates	1 1/2 tsp. cinnamon
1 1/4 cup brown sugar	1 pkg. mixed peel	1 cup butter	1 cup currants
1/2 cup mixed fruit	1/2 tsp. ginger	1/4 cup molasses	

Cream butter gradually and blend in sugar. Add unbeaten eggs one at a time. Beat well after each addition. Stir in molasses and add flour mixture after each addition. Add fruit and mix well. Put spices in flour. Place cake in angelfood pan lined with three layers of paper. Bake 2 1/2 hours to 3 1/2 hours at 300 F. Stand in pan until cold.

Mrs . W. Freake - Joe Batt' s Arm

RICH WEDDING CAKE

6 cups sultana raisins	6 cups seedless raisins	2 cups walnuts	3 tsp. baking powder
4 tsp. cinnamon	1 tsp. vanilla	12 egg yolks	3 cups currents
1/2 cup grapefruit juice	3 cups mixed peel	1 lb. butter	1/2 tsp. salt
1 tsp. nutmeg	1 tsp. almond	1/2 cup molasses	8 oz. dates
1/2 cup strong coffee	1/2 lb. cherries	3 1/2 cups flour	2 tsp. allspice
1/2 tsp. cloves	2 cups sugar	12 egg whites	

Grease 3 wedding cake pans, 4", 6", 8" in diameter; line with greased heavy brown paper. Combine fruits and nuts; dust with a little of the measured flour. Let stand overnight. Stir baking powder, salt, allspice, etc. and flour together. Cream butter, add sugar gradually, beating between additions. Add eggs and other liquids. Blend in dry ingredients; fold in floured fruits and nuts. Fill prepared pins 2/3 full. Bake in a slow oven (275 F.) 4 to 6 hours, depending on size or until done.

Mrs. Cyril Martin, St. Vincent' s, St. Mary' s Bay

BLUEBERRY COOKIES

1/2 cup shortening	1 1/2 cup flour	1/2 tsp. salt	1 cup brown sugar
1 tsp. baking powder	1/3 cup sour milk	2 eggs, beaten	1 tsp. baking soda
1 cup blueberries			

Cream shortening and sugar together. Add eggs, beaten until light & fluffy. Sift dry ingredients together and add to creamed mixture alternately with sour milk. Fold in blueberries. Drop from a tsp. on greased baking sheet. Bake in preheated 350 F. oven for about 12 minutes. Makes 4 dozen cookies.

"Blueberries are Mother Nature's convenience food. No peeling, no pitting, no coring. Just wash them and enjoy their flavour. Blueberries were probably the first familiar foodstuff the early colonists found in the New World. Sweet and succulent, their harvest soon became a familiar tradition throughout Newfoundland." Mrs. Frank Hollett, Blackhead.

BLUEBERRY GRUNT

1 cup butter	3 eggs	2 1/2 cups flour	3 tbs. baking powder
1 tsp. vanilla	1 cup sugar	blueberries	

Cream butter; add sugar gradually. Add eggs one at a time. Add vanilla and dry ingredients. Bake in hot oven.

GOLF BALLS

1/2 cup butter	1/2 cup milk	2 cups sugar

Boil above for 5 minutes & pour over 3 1/2 cups rolled oats, 1 1/2 cups coconut, 6 tbsp. cocoa & 1 tsp. vanilla mixed up. Roll in coconut.

United Church Women - St. John's

Bonfire night
November 5th.

Bonfire Night — Weeks and sometimes months of preparation is necessary for the proper celebration of 'Bonfire Night' on November 5th. Boys and girls make steadfast trips back into the woods to collect boughs for the great event. Boxes, tires, pailings and poles gradually become a small mountain of debris to be swallowed up in flame. Nor are outhouses and old punts secure from the hungry fire, for they have often gone up in smoke while unsuspecting owners slept. But fun is the name of the game and young ones are usually content to bake a potato or roast marshmallows in the hot coals.

MINCE MEAT COOKIES

1/4 cup fat (may use bacon)	1 cup flour + 2 tbsp.	1/4 tsp. salt	1/2 cup white sugar
1 egg	1 cup mincemeat	2 tsp. baking powder	

Cream fat, add sugar, egg and mincemeat. Mix thoroughly. Add sifted dry ingredients. Drop by spoon on cookie sheet and bake 12 to 15 minutes in 350 F. oven. Makes 2 dozen cookies.

Jessie Hooper, Churchill Falls, Labrador

PAROWAX COOKIES

1/2 block parowax	1 cup icing sugar	1 pk. choc. chips	5 cups corn flakes
1/2 cup peanut butter			

Melt parowax and chocolate chips. Add peanut butter and icing sugar. Stir in corn flakes. Drop on cookie sheet or wax paper to cool. Rice Krispies may be used in place of corn flakes.

Jessie Hooper, Churchill Falls, Labrador

LEMON SQUARES

2 cups flour	3/4 cup butter	2 cups cocoanut	1 tsp. baking powder
1 cup white sugar	1 pkg. lemon pie filling		

Press half dry ingredients in pan. Mix lemon and pour over lt. Put remainder of dry ingredients on top. Bake 35 to 40 min. at 350 F.

Mrs. Cyril Martin, St. Vincent's, St. Mary's Bay

GREAT GRANDMOTHER' S GINGER BREAD

1/2 cup butter or lard	1/2 cup sugar	1 egg, beaten	1 cup molasses
2 1/2 cups sifted flour	1 1/2 tsp. baking soda	1/2 tsp. salt	1 tsp cinnamon
1 tsp. ginger	1/2 tsp cloves	1 cup hot water	

Cream butter & sugar. Add beaten egg & molasses; beat well. Blend in sifted dry ingredients. Add hot water last & beat until smooth. Bake in a 9 inch square pan for 45 minutes. Use a 350 F oven.

"This recipe is well over 100 years old."   Mrs. Clara Temple of Sunnyside and Mary Frost of Hillview.

SOFT GINGERBREAD

1 egg, optional	2 tsp. ginger	1 cup boiling water	1 cup molasses
1 tsp. baking soda	2 cups bread flour	3 tbsp. butter	1/2 tsp. salt

Beat the egg; add molasses and the other ingredients in the order given. Melt the butter. Beat thoroughly and transfer to a well oiled pan about 9 inches square and bake from 40 to 50 minutes in a moderate oven (350 F.).   *Mrs. Gordon Hollett, Garden Cove.*

OLD TIME COOKIES

1/2 cup margarine	1 cup sugar	3 eggs, beaten	1 tsp. vanilla
2 3/4 cups flour	1 tsp. soda	1/2 tsp. salt	3/4 cup nuts
1/2 cup cherries	1 cup currants	cut up last 3 fruits	

Cream butter & sugar. Add eggs & vanilla. Sift together flour, soda, & salt. Blend nuts, cherries & currants. Mix fruit well with flour & add gradually to creamed mixture. Blend well. Drop by tsp. onto greased cookie sheet. Bake 8 -10 min.   *Mrs. Hilda Reid, Garden Cove.*

RAISIN AND NUT COOKIES

1/2 cup butter	1 cup flour	1 tsp. vanilla	1/4 cup sugar
1/4 tsp. salt	1/2 cup chopped walnuts	1 egg	1 tsp. baking powder
1/2 cup raisins			

Cream butter, sugar & egg together. Sift flour, salt and baking powder. Add this to the creamed mixture. Add vanilla, walnuts and raisins. Mix together. Drop by spoonfuls on a greased cookie sheet. Bake 15 min. at 350 F.

PEANUT BUTTER COOKIES

1 cup flour	1/2 tsp. salt	1/3 cup sugar	2 eggs
1 1/2 tsp. baking powder	2/3 cup butter	1 cup brown sugar	1/4 tsp. baking soda
1 cup peanut butter	1 tsp. vanilla		

Combine sifted flour, baking powder, baking soda and salt. Beat butter until it is creamy. Add peanut butter & continue beating until thoroughly blended. Gradually beat in sugar, brown sugar and vanilla. Add eggs and beat well. Stir in rolled oats & sifted flour mixture. Drop dough on ungreased baking sheet. Bake until done.

United Church Women - Fogo Island

MARSHMALLOW COOKIES

Beat 1 egg. Add 1 cup icing sugar, 2 squares chocolate melted or 6 tblspns. cocoa. Cut marshmallows in quarters & mix with above. Cover sheet of wax paper with cocoanut. Drop mixture on paper and roll to make log. Slice when cool. Coloured marshmallows are best.

Flora Primer, Barr'd Islands

APPLE CRISP

| 4 tbsp. butter | 8 tbsp. brown sugar | 12 tbsp. flour |

Mix together and put on top of sliced apples with nutmeg and bake in 350 F. oven until golden brown.

APPLE FILLING

| juice & rind of lemon | butter size of egg | 1 cup white sugar | 1 egg yolk |
| 1 apple, peeled & grated | | | |

Cook until thick. Cool, then put between layers and ice with butter icing. Keeps well.

Gladys Garland LowerIsland Cove,C.B., Nfld.

RICH DATE LOAF

3/4 cup butter	1 tsp. salt	1/2 cup warm water	1 cup sugar
1 cup graham flour	1 lb. dates	2 eggs	1 cup white flour
1 cup chopped walnuts	1 tsp. soda dissolved in water		

Cream butter and sugar. Add eggs. Pour the warm water and soda over dates and add with flour and salt mixture. Add walnuts and mix. Bake in moderate oven 45 minutes in loaf tin.

"This is an old recipe. I've given it to many. I'm sure everyone will like it."

Gladys Garland, Lower Island Cove, Nfld.

DELICIOUS NUT BARS

1/4 cup shortening	1/2 cup brown sugar	1 cup sifted all-purpose flour

Cream the shortening, gradually add the brown sugar, blend well. Sift in flour, stirring with a fork until the mixture is crumbly. Pat into an oiled pan 8 inches by 12 inches. Bake in a moderate oven for 12 or 15 minutes. Watch that the edges do not brown too much. As this is baking, proceed with the following:

2 eggs slightly beaten	1/2 cup nuts chopped	1/4 tsp. salt	1 tsp. vanilla
1/2 cup raisins chopped	1/2 tsp. baking powder	1 cup brown sugar	1 tbsp. corn starch
1 cup shredded cocoanut			

Mix together the slightly beaten eggs, sugar and vanilla. Add the remaining ingredients. Mix well. Pour over the partly baked shortbread foundation. Return to the oven and continue cooking for 25 minutes. While still warm, cut in bars. Yield — 30 bars. They are very good.

Mrs. Gladys Garland, Lower Island Cove, C.B., Nfld.

APRICOT NUT BREAD

1 cup flour	1 cup walnuts	3 tsp. baking powder	1/2 tsp. salt
1 cup dried apricots	2 tbsp. melted butter	1 egg slightly beaten	1 cup milk
1 cup white sugar	1 1/2 tsp. grated lemon rind		

Preheat oven to 350 F. Grease loaf pan. Sift together flour, baking powder, salt, baking soda and sugar. Stir in chopped up apricots, nuts and lemon rind. Add melted butter, egg and milk all at once and stir only enough to moisten dry ingredients then turn mixture into the prepared pan.

"This is an old, tried and true recipe, very easy and quick to make. Delicious for afternoon tea or supper bread."

Anne F. Snow, Clarkes Beach, Nfld.

BLACKBERRY BANG BELLY

bread	spices	flour	molasses
cinnamon	baking soda	salt Pork	cloves

Soak bread. Cut pork in very small squares. Add pork, molasses, spices, small amount of soda and blackberries to soaked bread. Also add enough flour, about 1 cupful, to make mixture not as soft. Drain water from bread before adding other ingredients; use amount of bread as needed and molasses to taste.

"Blackberry Bang Belly" originated from Dorcesetshire, England, and brought to Cape Freels, Newfoundland by the first settlers there. The recipe was enjoyed by old and young alike in early summer when the blackberries grew there in profusion. It was baked in a long rectangular pan. When cold, cut in slices, like a cake. Just try it!"

Joan Andrews, George's Brook, Nfld.

YUM - YUMS

Beat the yolk of 2 eggs and add:

1 cup brown sugar	2 tsp. baking powder	1/2 cup soft butter	1 tsp. vanilla
1 1/2 cups flour	1/4 tsp. salt		

Mix together, press in pan and bake to delicate brown about 10 minutes in 325 F. oven. Take out of oven and put 3/4 cup walnuts over mixture and then add 2 beaten egg whites and 1 cup brown sugar. Put back in oven until brown.

Mrs. Stella Collins - Stag Harbour, Nfld.

MARTHA WASHINGTON PIE

Take 4 ozs. blanched almonds and pound in a mortar with 2 ozs. powdered sugar, adding gradually 1 raw egg. When well pounded add:

1/2 gill rum	2 ozs. more of sugar	2 ozs. melted butter	another egg
1/2 tsp. ground cinnamon	6 drops orange flower water		

Pound for 5 minutes and add 2 ozs. well pounded macaroons. Line pie plate with good pastry, pour in preparation and bake. Decorate with candied fruits.

From "The New Cook Book" - 95 years old

Mrs. Eileen Thistle, Corner Brook, Nfld.

BAKEAPPLE PIE

2 cups bakeapples	2 tbsp. tapioca	1 cup sugar	Any favourite pastry recipe

Mix 2 cups bakeapples with 1 cup sugar, let stand while making pastry. Line bottom of pie-plate with the pastry, sprinkle with 2 tbsp. tapioca to absorb juice. Fill shell with bakeapples and sugar mixture, cover with pastry and proceed as with any berry pie. Serve with 'clotted cream' and you have a dish 'fit for a Queen'.

"Clotted cream is cream skimmed from milk that has been scalded and chilled. Bakeapples are yellow deliciously flavoured berries, which grow in boggy areas throughout Newfoundland and Labrador. An average serving is equivalent in vitamin C to an orange or half a grapefruit. It is said that when the French first came to our shores and found this unknown berry they said, "What is this berry?" or "Baie qu' appelle?" Hence comes the name bakeapple which is often confused by the stranger or foreigner with 'baked apple'."

CUT GLASS SQUARES

| 2 cups flour | 1/4 cup icing sugar | 1/2 cup butter |

Press in long angel food pan. Bake until brown. Let cool.

3 pks. jelly: lemon, lime & raspberry	1/4 cup cold water	2 envelopes gelatin
1 cup hot pineapple juice	1 tsp. vanilla	1/4 cup sugar
1 1/2 cups hot water for each pack of jelly.	1 tin cream	

Dissolve jelly each pack in separate dishes in hot water. Chill until firm. Cut in half inch cubes. Soften gelatine in cold water, then add to hot pineapple juice. Cool then fold in whipped cream mixture, into which you have beaten sugar and vanilla. Blend jelly cubes into whipped cream mixture. Spread on layer in pan. Top with dream whip. Chill until firm. Cut in squares.

"Dear sir, I am sending you a couple of my recipes which we like very much and I would like to share them by having them used in "Fat Back & Molasses."

Mrs. Doris Quinlan, Birchy Bay, Nfld

JELLY SQUARES

Line 8 inch square pan with graham wafers. Set one pack of jelly in 1 cup hot water. Let stand 20 minutes. Mix one pack dream whip, then mix the jelly with the dream whip. Spread on the wafers. Add another layer of wafers.

| **Icing**: 1/4 cup butter | 1 tbsp. flour | 1 tsp. vanilla | 1/4 cup sugar |
| 1 tbsp. milk | 1 tsp. hot water | | |

Beat together and put on wafers. Put in fridge. When set, cut in squares.

Mrs. Doris Quinlan, P.O. Box 54, Birchy Bay, Nfld. AOG 1EO

1, 2, 3, 4 CAKE

One cup butter; **two** cups sugar; **three** cups flour; **four** eggs. Add a little more flour if needed and roll out very thin on sugar. Cut any shape and bake quickly.

Mrs. Parmenas Wells, Fogo

SNOW BALLS

1 cup butter   2 cups flour   3/4 cup brown sugar   1 egg yolk

Mix then take small pieces of dough and flatten. Put cherry or dates in centre. Form into balls and bake. When cool, ice with icing sugar. Roll into coconut.

Mrs. Gladys Garland, Lower Island Cove, C.B., Nfld.

A TOAST

"Here's to the women; God created them beautiful and foolish. Beautiful so the men would love them; foolish so they would love the men."

Submitted by Mrs. Florence Wilkinson-Moores

Have you read all the recipes in our book?
We hope you've found some Goodies to cook.
Our wishes for you are most sincere
for Blessings and Happiness year after year.

MARBLE COOKIES

1/3 cup butter	1 cup flour	1 tsp. vanilla	1 cup sugar
1/2 tsp. baking powder	2 eggs	1/2 cup coconut	
2 - 1 oz. squares unsweetened chocolate			

Cream butter and sugar. Add eggs and beat well. Measure flour and baking powder on paper. Stir into cream mixture coconut and vanilla. Then divide batter into half. Add melted chocolate to 1/2 of batter. Drop the batter by tsp. into square cookie pan, mixing the dark through the light. Bake for 20 minutes at 350 F. Cool. Add icing sugar to top. These cookies are quite good!

Jessie Hooper, Churchill Falls, Labrador

BUTTER SCOTCH SQUARES

Put on stove and melt 1 cup butter or margarine and 2 cups brown sugar. Then add in 1 tsp. baking soda and mix well. Add 4 cups rolled oats. Bake in moderate oven about 350 to 375 F. about 25 minutes. The cake comes out all bubbly. Cut in squares right away.

Mrs. G. Iwanonkiw, Thunder Bay, Ontario.

HOMEMADE ICING

1/2 cup white sugar	6 tbsp. milk	1 cup butter	6 tbsp. hot water
6 tbsp. flour	1 tsp. vanilla		

Beat at high speed until fluffy.

Mrs. Rosalind Fraser, Sudbury, Ont. (Bishop's Falls)

BANANA LOAF

Sift: 1/4 tsp. baking soda   1 3/4 cups flour   1/2 tsp. salt   2 tsp. baking powder

Cream: 1/3 cup margarine. Beat in 2/3 cup sugar. Add 2 beaten eggs. Add dry ingredients with 1 cup mashed banana. Pour in greased loaf pan. Let stand 20 minutes. Bake at 350 F. for 50 - 55 minutes.

Mrs. Rosalind Fraser, Sudbury, Ont. (Bishop's Falls)

RECIPE FOR SPRUCE BEER

There are two kinds of spruce trees that grow in Newfoundland - White Spruce and Black Spruce. White Spruce is known to be poisonous - the Black variety is used to make Spruce Beer.

1 bunch black spruce bushes   molasses, according to desired amount of beer   1 cup sugar
1 boiler (about 3/4 full of water)   2 pkgs. Fleischmann's dry yeast   1 cup apricots or raisins

Boil a bunch of black spruce bushes for approximately 2 hours. Strain the water off the bushes and add more if necessary. To prevent beer from being bitter, have a greater amount of warm water than spruce bush water. Add yeast and molasses; also add sugar and apricots or raisins. Mix all ingredients together. Cork mixture in a jar and let brew for about 2 1/2 days or longer in cold weather. Open and serve.

Note: Increase amount of ingredients in accordance with the size of brewing utensil used. Beer can also be made by boiling spruce buds in a calico bag in the same manner and using the same ingredients.

Bride Whiffen Southern Harbour, Placentia Bay

SAUCEPAN COOKIES

1/2 cup butter   1/2 cup chopped walnuts   3/4 cup sugar   1 tsp. salt
2 eggs   1 cup chopped dates

Cook over low heat for ten minutes. Remove from heat and add 1 tsp. vanilla. Cool for about 5 minutes and then fold in 2 cups crisp rice cereal. Form into balls and roll in coconut.

Mrs. Dorcas Leyte - Fogo

PUDDING COOKIES

1 pkg. vanilla instant pudding   3/4 cup biscuit mix   1 egg   1/4 cup salad oil
1 tsp. vanilla

Shape into balls after combining and mixing the above ingredients. Place on ungreased cookie sheets. Flatten with fork. Bake at 350 F. for 10 - 15 min.

Mrs. Alma Payne - Fogo

BLACK AND WHITE COOKIES

Underlayer: Mix 1 pkg. graham wafer biscuits & 1 cup of butter.

Middle layer: Mix together 1 tin sweetened milk, 2 cups cocoanut, place on top of underlayer and bake until golden brown. Mix icing sugar and cocoa for icing and place on top of cookies after baking.

CHOCOLATE CRACKERS

1 pkg. sweetened chocolate, 2 cups corn flakes. Melt chocolate in double boiler allowing it not to get too hot. Add corn flakes and stir. Drop on waxed paper. Allow to cool and harden.

Cynthia Coish - Stagg Harbour

RAISIN DROP COOKIES

2 cups seeded raisins	1 cup water	1 tsp. baking soda	2 cups brown sugar
1 cup walnuts if desired	1 cup butter or shortening	1 tsp. vanilla	3 eggs well beaten
4 cups flour	1 tsp. baking powder	1/2 tsp. salt	1/4 tsp. nutmeg
1 tsp. cinnamon			

Add water to raisins, boil briskly for about 5 minutes. Cool, stirring in baking soda and let stand. Cream shortening and sugar until light and fluffy. Add vanilla, beaten egg and cooled raisins with their liquid. Then mix with flour sifted with baking powder and salt. Drop from teaspoon on baking sheet. Bake in moderate oven. If preferred, these cookies may be spread on cookie sheet and cut in squares when cooled.

"The above recipe has been one of our favourite cookie recipes for a long time, both in our parents home and with my own family. They are not dainty cookies, but the kind that the common folks enjoy."
Mrs. Carry Eddy, North Harbour

JELLY ROLL

1/3 cup shortening	1 tspn. salt	2 tspn. baking powder	1 cup sugar
1/2 cup cold water	jelly or jam	3 eggs	1 1/4 cups flour

Cream shortening, salt & sugar. Add beaten egg yolks, water and then add alternately flour, sifted with baking powder & beaten egg whites. Pour into shallow baking pan lined with wax paper. Bake in hot oven. Turn from pan on to a towel, trip edges, spread with jelly. Roll up in the towel while warm. Let stand a few minutes, then dust with powdered sugar.

"The origin of this recipe is that it was taken from 'Miss Olive Allen's book of Tested Recipes'. My special recollection of it is that it was served at my wedding over 30 years ago. It is a fact too, that it has been served at many suppers and bazaars in our United Church at Sound Isld. long before that, and many many times since that at Garden Cove."
Mrs. Ernest Hollett, Garden Cove

NO BAKE CHOCOLATE CREAM COOKIES

1/2 cup butter	1 tsp. vanilla	1 cup coconut	1 tsp. milk or cream
1/2 tin of sweetened condensed milk (15 oz.)		1 envelope chocolate	1 egg beaten
1/2 cup nuts	2 cups sifted icing sugar	1/4 cup gran. sugar	1 tsp. vanilla
1/4 cup soft butter	2 cups graham wafer crumbs		

Melt 1/2 cup butter in saucepan. Remove from heat & add 1 envelope liquid unsweetened chocolate. Blend in sugar, 1 tsp. vanilla, eggs, wafers, coconut & nuts into buttered chocolate mixture. Mix well & press into ungreased pan. Chill.

Melt 1/4 cup butter, milk or cream, icing sugar & 1 tsp. vanilla. Spread over crumbs mixture and chill.

Mix 1 envelope liquid unsweetened chocolate & sweetened condensed milk in a saucepan and gradually heat. Spread a thin layer of this mixture on top of chilled filling. Return to refrigerator to set. Cut into squares before completely firm. Yields 3 to 4 dozen.

Mrs. Manuel Reid - Barr'd Islands

CARAMEL NUT COOKIES

Sift together:	3 1/2 cups flour, 1 tsp. baking soda, 1/2 tsp. salt & set aside.
Work with a spoon until soft:	1 cup butter or margarine.
Add gradually while beating:	2 cups brown sugar & beat until light. Add 2 eggs & beat until light & slubby.
Gradually add dry ingredients:	Mix well after each addition - 1 cup finely chopped walnuts. Mix well and shape into balls.

Bake until done, about 8 to 10 minutes.

Mrs. A. Payne - Fogo

COOKIES

1/2 cup sugar	1/2 up butter	**Topping**
1 tsp. baking powder	1 egg	1 cup pineapple juice
2 cups flour		1 pkg. gelatine

Cream butter, sugar and egg and rub in flour and baking powder. Press in pan and bake until brown. Cool. Heat topping until all melted, then cool. Beat Dream Whip as instruction given, then beat in juice and gelatine. Cut up jelly and mix it in. Place on batter. Cool and cut in squares.

United Church Women - Fogo Island

DROP COOKIES

1 cup brown sugar	1 tsp. cinnamon	1/2 cup molasses	1/2 cup walnut
1 1/2 cups flour	1 tsp. nutmeg	1/2 cup shortening	1/2 cup raisins
1 egg	1/2 tsp. salt	1 level tsp. soda dissolved in 1/4 cup hot water	

Blend in usual manner and drop by spoonfulls on greased sheet. Bake at 350 F.

RUBY COOKIES

3/4 cup melted butter   21 graham wafers crushed fine.
Mix above together and place in square pan & bake at 350 F. for 10 minutes.

1 can condensed milk   2 cups coconut
Combine above and place on top of first mixture while warm. Place in oven and brown. Frost with chocolate icing.

Mrs. Alex Hynes - Stag

CENTENNIAL COOKIES

1 pkg. semi sweet choc. chips	1/4 cup brown sugar	1 1/2 cups small marshmallows
1/2 cup melted butter	1 1/2 cups graham wafers	1 tin cream
1 pkg. dream whip mixed with 3/4 cup milk		

Melt chocolate chips in double boiler over hot water & cool. Crush graham wafers very fine. Add brown sugar to wafer crumbs. Add the 1/2 cup melted butter. Mix together. Take half and press into 8" square pan. Beat dream whip stiff. Add cream and beat again. Take half the cream mixture and add the chocolate chips melted and beat together. Stir in marshmallows and spread over first layer. (press) Take remaining cream and spread on the third layer. Sprinkle with coconut. Keep in a cool place.

United Church Women - Fogo

ICE CREAM COOKIES

24 Graham crackers	1 tsp. vanilla	2 tsp. brown sugar	1/2 cup melted butter

Mix above & spread in 8" sq. pan. Save 1/4 cup of this mixture for topping.

1/2 cup butter	2 squares bakers chocolate (semi-sweet)	2 cups icing sugar
2 well beaten eggs	1 1/2 cups fine cocoanut	

Spread over bottom mixture and put in refrigerator.

Mrs. Douglas Freake - Joe Batt's Arm

LIGHT PATTY

3/4 cup butter	2 eggs	1 cup milk	1/4 cup shortening
1 tsp. vanilla	1 cup cherries cut up	2 cups flour	1 cup white sugar

Cream butter & shortening. Add sugar. Beat in eggs. Add vanilla, cherries & flour. Bake 20 minutes.

Mrs. Dorcas Leyte - Fogo

PEACH - RICE LOAF SUPREME

28 oz. can sliced peaches	2 tbsp. cornstarch	1 tsp. almond extract	3/4 cup sugar
1 cup fine graham wafer crumbs	1 1/2 cups milk	1/2 tsp. vanilla	1/4 tsp. salt
2 egg yolks, beaten	2 cups cooked rice		

Heat oven to 350 F. and butter a glass dish. Drain peaches & save juice for sauce. Combine sugar, cornstarch & salt in saucepan. Add milk. Boil for 1 minute & add a little of the hot mixture to egg yolks. Remove from heat and add almond, vanilla and rice.

Spread graham crumbs over bottom of the dish. Spread 1/3 rice mixture, then 1/2 the peach slices, then the other 1/3 rice mixture and the remaining peaches and top with the remaining rice. Sprinkle the remaining graham crumbs. Bake 40 minutes.

Mrs. Ethel Anthony - Seldom Come By

RICE KRISPIE COOKIES

Put in a saucepan and mix 1/2 cup butter, 1 cup sugar, 1 cup dates and bring to a boil. Stir in one egg and cook 10 minutes. Let cool. Stir in 2 or 3 cups of rice Krispies. Roll in balls. Then roll in coconut. Add walnuts if desired.

Mrs. Alvie Brown - Joe Batt's Arm

COFFEE CAKE

One cup of molasses, one cup of brown sugar, one cup cold coffee, four cups sifted flour, half cup of butter, small teaspoon of allspice, two tsp. baking powder. Mix together and bake in moderate oven.

United Church Women - Fogo

BLUEBERRY CRUNCH

2 cups blueberries	1 cup brown sugar	1/2 cup butter	1/2 cup white sugar
1/4 tsp. salt	1 cup flour	1/2 tsp. cinnamon	

Put blueberries in 8 inch square baking dish and sprinkle with 1/2 cup of white sugar. Mix together flour, brown sugar, salt and cinnamon. Cut butter into flour mixture until crumbly. Sprinkle this mixture over berries and bake at 350 F. for 30 minutes.

BLUEBERRY CAKE

1 cup sugar	1/3 cup butter	1 cup blueberries	1 1/2 cups flour
1/2 cup milk	2 tsp. baking powder	2 eggs	few grains salt
1 tsp. lemon flavouring			

Cream butter thoroughly and add the sugar gradually. Cream together well. Add well beaten egg. Sift flour 3 times, baking powder and salt. Add flour alternately with milk. Add flavouring. Add berries and mix lightly. Pour into a greased loaf pan and bake in a moderate oven for 45 minutes.

BLUEBERRY SQUARES

3 tbsp. butter	2/3 cup flour	1/4 cup milk	1/3 cup sugar
1 tsp. baking powder	1/4 tsp. vanilla	2 egg yolks	1/4 tsp. salt

Cream butter and sugar, beat in egg yolks. Add sifted dry ingredients alternately with milk and vanilla. Pour into greased 8" square pan. Bake at 350 F. for 18 - 20 minutes.

Topping for above squares: Beat 2 egg whites until peaked. Beat in 6 tbsp. sugar, 1/4 tsp. salt and fold in 1 cup of fresh blueberries. Spread over baked cake portion. Return to oven heated to 300 F. Bake until topping has browned slightly (12 to 15 minutes).

The above Blueberry recipes are from the "Labrador Cookbook"

ROLLS

Make a sponge of 1 pint milk (lukewarm), 2 tbsp. sugar, 2 tbsp. butter, 1 yeast cake dissolved in 1/2 cup lukewarm water and thicken with flour and 1 tsp. salt. When risen, add 1 egg and enough flour to knead. Set to rise again. Knead when risen and put in desired shapes. Let rise and bake until brown.

Mrs. Bernice Hynes - Stag Harbour

DATE SQUARES

1 3/4 cups flour
1 cup butter
2 cups rolled oats

1/2 tsp. soda
1 1/2 cups water
1 cup brown sugar

Filling
1 1/2 cups dates
1/2 cup white sugar

Spread date mixture over rolled oats mixture. Top with remaining mixture. Bake in oven 350 F. until light brown.

Mrs. Daisy Brown - Fogo

CARAMEL SQUARES

1/2 cup butter
1/2 tsp. vanilla
1 3/4 cups flour

1/2 cup brown sugar
1 egg yolk

Filling
1 egg white
1 cup walnuts
1 cup brown sugar

Cream butter and sugar with egg. Beat well. Beat this topping together.

Mrs. M. Johnson, North Hr. & Mrs. Daisy Brown - Fogo

RHUBARB-MARSHMALLOW DESSERT

1 cup stewed rhubarb drained   1 cup whipped cream   16 large marshmallows
1/2 cup rhubarb juice

Place rhubarb juice and marshmallow in top of double boiler and heat over simmering water till melted. Blend well. Add drained rhubarb and fold in cold. Do not chill. Whip cream until fluffy and fold in. Chill. (serves 6)

United Church Women - Fogo Island

PINEAPPLE SURPRISES

1/2 cup butter   pineapple cubes well drained   1 cup icing sugar   1 tsp. vanilla
2 cups coconut   Graham wafer crumbs.

Cream butter and sugar. Add coconut and vanilla. Mould around pineapple cube and roll in Graham wafer crumbs.

United Church Women - Fogo Island

MOLASSES TARTS

1 1/2 cups butter or shortening   4 cups flour   2 tsp. spice   2 tsp. cinnamon
2 tsp. soda dissolved in 1/4 cup tea   1 1/2 cups molasses   2 tsp. cloves

Mix all ingredients together well and 'patty' mixture on pie plate. Fill with any jam desired & arrange pastry strips across top. Bake in moderate oven until done. This recipe makes several tarts.
Note: the above recipe is another Newfoundland favourite.

Mrs. Alex Hynes - Stag Harb

PUMPKIN MARMALADE

6 lb. pumpkin	1 tin crushed pineapple	4 1/2 lb. sugar	2 lemons or oranges

Vegetable marrow may be used instead of pumpkin

Peel pumpkin or vegetable marrow. Remove seeds and pulp and cut up fine. Add sugar and set aside for 2 days. Add lemon and rind. Cut fine and boil for 8 hours slowly and very rapidly for the last 10 minutes. Add pineapple last.

"The history of the above recipe, as far as I can learn, is that it originated about 40 or 50 years ago. It was made use of by my husband's grandmother and her family on many occasions, as it was a favourite marmalade. They used to grow the pumpkins and vegetable marrows at that time. Many's a jar of the delicacy found its way to the Harvest Festivals and Church Bazaars in those days."

Mrs. George Hollett, Garden Cove

BRANBURY TARTS

1/2 up seedless raisins	juice of 1 lemon	1/2 up dried currants	1 egg
Grated rind of 1 lemon	1 cup sugar	1/4 cup cracker crumbs	

Mix together the fruit, sugar, lemon juice, cracker crumbs and grated rind. Beat the egg and add it stirring it in thoroughly. Roll plain pastry (your usual recipe) to one eighth of an inch thick.

Cut with round cutter. Put a tablespoon of the mixture on one round & cover it with another. Dampen fingers & pinch edges together. Prick the centre of each with a fork and bake in a hot oven 450 F. for about 20 minutes or until light brown.

These are delicious and different."

Mrs. Florence Wilkinson-Moores, Topsail

PEACH SQUARES

1/2 cup butter   1 cup coconut   3/4 cup sugar   1 unbeaten egg
1 tin sliced peaches, drained and mashed.

Cream together butter and sugar. Add unbeaten egg, coconut and peaches. Line 6" by 9" pan with Graham Wafers. Put filling over this then add another layer of wafers. Whip one pkg. Dream Whip and put on top, then sprinkle with coconut. Leave in refrigerator until cool. Cut in squares.

Recipe from Mrs. Roy Anthony, Seldom Come By and Martha Hewitt, Barr'd Islands.

ORANGE SQUARES

2 cups sifted flour   3/4 cup granulated sugar   1/2 tsp. salt   2 cups coconut
1 tsp. baking powder   1 cup butter

Sift dry ingredients together. Add coconut. Rub in butter until mixture is crumbly. Press half of this mixture over bottom of a greased pan about 9" square. **For the filling combine** - 1 cup granulated sugar, 2 teaspoons custard powder (or more), 1 orange (juice, pulp & grated rind) & 1 cup of water. Boil filling until it thickens, then add 1 tbsp. butter & spread over layer of crumbs in the pan. Bake at 350 F. for 25 to 30 minutes. Cut in squares when cool.

Mrs. Maud Freake - Joe Batt's Arm, Nfld.

MOLASSES TAFFY

2 cups molasses   1 cup sugar   1 tbsp. vinegar   2 tbs. butter
Place all ingredients in a saucepan. Boil until mixture becomes brittle — hard crack stage (when a drop put in cold water forms a ball), pour into buttered pan. Grease hands and when cool enough to handle, pull the toffee until it becomes light in colour. Cut into pieces with scissors.

ICE CREAM SQUARES

2 cups graham waf. crumbs   1/2 cup butter   1 pkg. jelly (any kind)
1 brick vanilla ice cream

Save 1/4 cup crumbs for top of squares. Mix crumbs & butter. Take 1 cup boiling water & mix with jello until dissolved. Add ice cream until smooth and pour over crumb mixture. Sprinke crumbs on top. Put in refrigerator until set.

Betty Kinden - Stag Harbour

CARAMEL SAUCE

2 egg yolks   1/4 cup soft butter   1 cup brown sugar   1 tsp. vanilla
1/2 cup water

Beat eggs lightly with fork in top of a double boiler. Stir in sugar, water and butter. Set over boiling water and cook. Stir until thickened. Stir in vanilla and serve hot.

Mrs. Claude Gill - Fogo

BROWN SUGAR CANDY

2 cups brown sugar   1/3 cup milk   1 tbsp. butter   3/4 cup chopped nuts
1 tsp. vanilla

Put sugar, milk & butter into saucepan. Boil with as little stirring as possible until it makes a soft ball when tested in cold water. Take from fire and add nuts and vanilla. Beat until thick and pour into greased tins.

Mrs. Hubert Freake, Fogo

COCKTAIL SQUARES

Mix 30 single Graham crackers and 1/2 cup butter & spread on bottom of pan & bake 20 minutes at 325 F. Cool. For the TOP: use 1 large tin of fruit cocktail well drained, 1 tin Eagle Brand milk & the juice of 1 lemon. Mix fruit, milk, lemon together & spread over cooled crust. Bake 20 minutes at 325 F. Cool. Spread over with whipped cream or Dream Whip. Sprinkle with graham crackers broken up & keep in refrigerator.

United Church Women - Fogo Island.

CHRISTMAS DOMINOES

1/2 cup butter	1 cup coconut	1/2 cup sugar	1/2 cup chopped walnuts
2 cups graham wafers crushed	1 tsp. vanilla	1/3 cup cocoa	1 beaten egg

Combine all ingredients. Pour into greased 6" by 10" pan. Then combine 1/4 up butter, 2 tsp. vanilla & 2 cups sifted icing sugar. Spread over bottom layer in pan & chill.

United Church Women - Stag Harbour

ICE CREAM DELIGHTS

Mix 1 cup shortening, 1/4 tsp. salt, 3 tbsp. icing sugar & 1 cup flour. Press in 8" by 8" pan. Dissolve 1 pkg. lime jello in 1 cup boiling water. Pour into this mixture 1 pint vanilla ice-cream. Pour over first mixture & set in refrigerator. Cut in squares.

United Church Women - Fogo

LEMON SQUARES

25 Graham wafers rolled fine   2 tbsp. butter   1 tsp. vanilla

Mix thoroughly & save half of mixture for top. Pack in 9" by 9" pan.
For second layer: 1 can sweetened milk, 3 egg yolks, juice of 2 lemons. Add 2 stiffly beaten egg whites last. Pour over bottom layer & cover with remaining crumbs. Bake in 350 F. oven until brown.

Mrs. Verley Hewitt,; - Barr'd Islands.

STRAWBERRY SQUARES

Bottom: 2 1/2 cups Graham wafers crushed, mixed well with 1/2 cup butter. Press in pan.

Filling: 1 tub fresh strawberries; 1 pkg. strawberry jelly & 1 tsp. lemon juice. Bring to a boil, let cool, then pour over bottom & let set in fridge.

Top: With 1 pkg. Dream Whip. Put back in fridge until ready to serve.

Louise Decker - Joe Batt's Arm

MALTED MILK SQUARES

Line pan 9" by 13" with Graham Wafers. Mix 1/2 cup butter & 1/2 cup sugar & cream well. Add 2 eggs, 1 cup coconut, 2 tbsp. cocoa mixed with a little melted, butter. Spread on Graham Wafers. Cover all this with another layer of wafers. Top with Dream Whip.

United Church Women - Fogo Islan

CHOCOLATE COCONUT SQUARES

Bottom: 1 cup white sugar   2 egg yolks   2 tbsp. butter   1 tsp. baking powder
1 cup milk   1/2 cup coconut   1 cup flour

Put above in square pan & bake for 20 minutes.

Top: 2 egg whites (beaten stiff)   2 cups coconut   1/2 cup white sugar

Spread over partly baked bottom & return to oven for 30 minutes or until brown. Ice while warm with chocolate icing. Cut in squares.   *Mrs. Winston Bixby - Stagg Harbour*

MARSHMALLOW SQUARES

1 cup white sugar   2 eggs   1 cup margarine

Mix above in saucepan, cook on medium heat until mixture starts to bubble. Remove from stove and add the following:

1 tsp. almond extract   1/2 cup coconut   1/2 cup chopped nuts
24 Graham Wafers crushed coarsely.   2 cups small marshmallows

Flatten this mixture in an 8" by 8" pan & spread with chocolate icing. Chill well & cut as used. Keeps indefinitely.   *Mrs. Claude Gill - Fogo*

BROWNIES

3/4 cup brown sugar   3 tbsp. cocoa   1/2 tsp. baking powder   1/4 cup margarine
1/2 tsp. vanilla   1 egg   1/2 cup chopped walnuts   1/2 cup of flour

Cream brown sugar and margarine then beat in egg. Stir in flour, baking powder and cocoa, then add vanilla and chopped nuts. Put in greased square pan and bake at 350 F. until done. Ice while warm & cut into squares.   *Mrs. Lillian King - Millertown*

MARSHMALLOW SQUARES

2 cups graham wafers	32 marshmallows quartered	1 tsp. vanilla
1/3 cup cherries cut up	1 1/2 cups coconut	1/4 tsp. salt
1 1/3 cups sweetened condensed milk		

Blend marshmallows, sweetened milk, graham wafers, salt, vanilla & cherries. Line 8" by 8" pan with half the coconut. Add the marshmallow mixture & press down. Sprinkle remaining cocoanut on top. Press down. Place in refrigerator for 24 hours. Cut in squares with wet knife.

United Church Women - Fogo Island

APRICOT BARS

1 1/2 cups sifted flour	1/2 tsp. nutmeg	1 1/2 cups rolled oats	1 tsp. baking powder
1 cup brown sugar	1/2 tsp. salt	3/4 cup butter	

Heat oven to 375 F. Lightly grease a 13" by 9" by 2" pan. Sift flour, baking powder, salt & nutmeg into bowl. Add brown sugar & mix with a fork. Add butter & cut in with pastry blender. Add rolled oats & mix until crumbly. Put 2/3 of mixture into prepared pan & press down. Spread with apricot filling. Sprinkle remaining crumbs over filling. Bake about 35 minutes or until brown. Cut in squares while warm, but let cool in pan.

United Church Women - Fogo Island

APRICOT FILLING

3 cups dried apricots	1 1/2 cups water	3/4 cup sugar

Combine apricots and water in sauce pan. Cover & cook until apricots are tender & most of the water absorbed. Add sugar & cook uncovered stirring often, until thick. For sweeter filling, increase sugar to 1 cup.

United Church Women - Fogo

MALTED MILK SQUARES

Line pan with whole caramel wafers. **Filling**: mix 1/2 cup butter, 1/2 cup sugar, 2 eggs, 1 cup coconut, 2 tbsp. cocoa with a little melted butter. Spoon on the caramel wafers & cover with another layer of whole caramel wafers. Top with Dream Whip and chill.

United Church Women - Fogo Island

CHERRY CHEWS

1 cup butter	1 cup rolled oats	1 cup brown sugar	1 tsp. baking soda
1 cup flour	1/4 tsp. salt		

Press above in pan & bake 10 minutes.

2 eggs beaten	1 tsp. baking powder	1/2 cup walnuts	1 cup brown sugar
1/2 tsp. salt	1/2 cup cherries (cut fine)	2 tbsp. flour	1 cup coconut

Spread above on pastry & bake 20 minutes until brown. Cut in squares.

United Church Women - Fogo Island

MAIDS OF HONOUR

1/2 cup butter	2 cups flour	2 tbsp. icing sugar	jam

Mix the first 3 ingredients & put into muffin tins. Add about 1 tsp. of jam in each.

2 eggs	1 cup white sugar	2 tbsp. melted butter	1 cup coconut

Filling is made by beating the eggs until smooth. Add sugar, melted butter and coconut. Put on top of bottom layer & jam on each muffin. Bake in 350 F. for 25 minutes.

Mrs. Bride Sheppard - Stag Harbou

JELLY ROLL

3 eggs separated	1/2 tsp. vanilla or lemon extract	1 cup granulated sugar	1 cup flour
1 tsp. baking powder	1 tbsp. cold water	1/4 tsp. salt	

Beat egg whites until soft peaks start to form; gradually add sugar and beat until stiff, but not dry. Beat egg yolks until thick; add cold water and flavouring. Fold the beaten yolks into the egg whites; then fold in sifted dry ingredients.

Line bottom of shallow pan about 10" by 15" with waxed paper. Pour in batter and spread evenly. Bake at 400 F. for 12 to 15 minutes. Turn out on a towel which has been dusted with sugar. Remove wax paper and trip the edges. Spread with jam or jelly. Roll up. Wrap in waxed paper until serving time.

Mrs. Joan Brown - Joe Batt's Arm

DATE ROLLS

1 cup butter	1/2 cup coconut	1 cup brown sugar	1 1/2 cups flour

Roll in dates and bake for 10 minutes.

Mrs. Julia Leyte & Mrs. Daisy Brown, Fogo Island

CHRISTMAS BALLS

30 marshmallows	1 - 15 oz. can sweetened condensed milk	2 cups wafer crumbs
1/2 cup red cherries (halved)	1/2 cup green cherries	

Mix the above ingredients together.

Daisy Brown - Fogo

FEATHERBEDS

2 cups scalded milk	2 well beaten eggs	4 tbsp. butter	4 cups bread flour
1 1/2 tsp. salt	4 tbsp. sugar	1 pkg. yeast	

Melt butter in warm milk. Add salt, sugar & yeast cake. Dissolve in warm water and add eggs and flour. Beat well. Let rise until very light - about 2 hours in a warm place. Beat again. Place in buttered muffin tins about 3/4 full. Let rise again and bake in hot oven 450 F. for about 20 minutes.

Mrs. Parmenas Wells - Fogo

TEA SCONES

2 cups sifted flour	1/2 tsp. salt	2 tbsp. sugar	6 tbsp. butter
1 slightly beaten egg	3 tsp. baking powder	1/2 cup milk	

Sift together dry ingredients. Cut in butter till mixture resembles coarse crumbs. Add egg and milk, stirring only till dough follows fork around bowl. Turn out on floured surface. Knead gently about 15 times. Cut dough in half. Shape each half into a ball and pat or roll around about 1/2" thick and 6" in diameter. Cut into 8 wedges like a pie. Place the wedges on an ungreased baking sheet without allowing the sides to touch. Brush with slightly beaten egg. Bake at 425 F. about 12 to 15 minutes or until deep golden brown. (makes 16)

Mrs. Stella Decker - Joe Batt's Arm

CHOCOLATE CREAM

Dissolve half a cake of chocolate in a little hot water; put in a cup of milk, and when it boils have five eggs well beaten and mixed with two cups of milk; pour the hot chocolate into the eggs and milk; stir well and boil all together for a few minutes. Sweeten to your taste and eat cold.

Mrs. Parmenas Wells - Fogo

BUTTER BALLS

1 cup butter	2 3/4 cups flour	1 cup finely chopped nuts	1/2 cup sugar
1/4 tsp. salt	2 egg yolks	1 tsp. baking powder	

Mix all ingredients together except nuts, then roll in slightly beaten egg white and chopped nuts. Place on cookie sheet and make indentation in middle of cookie. Bake at 325 F. for 25 minutes. When cool, fill with jelly.

Mrs. Emma Keats, Barr'd Islands

MOLASSES STEAM PUDDING

1/2 cup butter	1 tsp. soda	1 egg	2 cups flour
3/4 cup molasses	1/4 cup white sugar	1/3 cup milk	salt
1 tsp. cinnamon			

Cream butter, sugar. Add egg & molasses & cream well. Stir in dry ingredients. Place in a double boiler and steam about 2 hours.

Mrs. Bernice Loder, Hillview, T. Bay, Nfld.

DATE COCONUT MACAROONS

2/3 cup sweet condensed milk	1 tsp. vanilla	1 cup each coconut, chopped nuts & dates

Heat oven to 350 F. Combine all ingredients. Drop by teaspoon 1" apart on greased cookie sheet. Bake 10-12 minutes.

Mrs. M. Best - Fogo

NEWFOUNDLAND WISDOM: "Waste neither time nor thought
About the bridge you'll never cross."

Mrs. Florence Wilkinson-Moores, Topsail

BLACKBERRY AND APPLE JAM

4 lb. blackberries	5 lb. sugar (more if needed)	1/2 pint water	1 1/2 lb. peeled,cored & sliced apples.

Place berries in a pan over low heat, adding half the quantity of water and stew slowly until tender. Stew the apples until soft in the remaining water. Combine the fruit, add the sugar and stir until dissolved and boil rapidly until settling point is reached.

United Church Women - Fogo Island

LASSIE POP

Boil 2 or 3 cups of molasses constantly until it forms a ball when dropped in cold water. Stir frequently to prevent burning or boiling over. When cooked enough throw on a well-greased platter until cool, then with buttered hands, (greased) stretch molasses into a long string. Must be done in a cool place. When stretched enough , twist, dip in cold water, then break into candy-sized pieces.

"This is an old family recipe, one much loved by children. Sometimes a few drops of peppermint would be dropped into the molasses while cooking. This was very helpful to coughs and colds."

Mrs. Jacob Best, Wesleyville, B. B. Nfld.

JAM JAMS

1 cup butter	1 egg	1 tsp. vanilla	1 tsp. soda
1/2 cup molasses	3 cups flour (more if needed)	1 cup brown sugar	3 tbsp. boiling water

Cream butter & sugar together until very creamy. Add egg & beat well. Dissolve molasses, soda & boiling water then add to mixture. Then add vanilla and flour. Mix all together. Roll on board & cut with cookie cutter. Bake about 15 minutes at 350 F. When baked put jam between two.

"This recipe was given to me by my Grandfather and it was used by all our families over the years. It's great to add to lunches for lunchboxes."

Mrs. Alma Loder - Hillview U.C.W.

DANDELION WINE

1 gal. dandelion water	1 pkg. yeast	1 orange	3 lbs. sugar
juice of 3 lemons	1 slice toast		

Pour the boiling water over well washed dandelion flowers & let stand over night. Strain & add lemon juice, orange juice and sugar. Chill for 1/2 hour. When cool add yeast spread on slice of toast. Let stand until fermentation ceases. Strain, bottle & cork well.

"This wine or even boiled dandelion was considered a 'tonic' in the springtime when folks were 'run down'. The standard of living was often anything but good with many people, and any home made tonic was welcome. Some folks kept it stored for a year or two (those who were getting their vitamins) which made it more palatable and perhaps decidedly intoxicating if taken in large amounts. Thus it serves a two-fold purpose as medicine and merry making."

Mrs. Mabel Squires, Blackhead U.C.W., Conception Bay

RICE WINE

3 lb. rice	1 oz. yeast	1 lb. raisins	5 qts. water	3 lb. sugar

Bring the water to boiling point and cut off the heat at once. Pour in the sugar & stir until dissolved. Then add the rice & chopped raisins. Allow the mixture to cool & sprinkle the yeast on top & stir in. After 14 days fermentation strain & proceed with isinglass & bottling.

"This recipe is more than 100 years old."

Mrs. Mae Mourton, Burin Bay Arm

NEWFOUNDLAND SAYING: "You can cut a notch in the Beam." Said when someone does the unusual.

Annie Hodder, Collins Cove, Burin

PARTRIDGEBERRY PUNCH

1 qt. partridgeberries	3 tbsp. lemon juice	1 cup orange juice	2 cups sugar
6 cups water	1 qt. ginger ale		

Cook partridgeberries in 4 cups water until soft. Crush & drain through cheesecloth. Boil sugar & remaining 2 cups water 5 minutes. Add to partridgeberry juice and chill. Add fruit juices. Just before serving add ginger ale.

Jubilee Guild of Nfld. & Lab.

APRICOT BRANDY

Let 2 lbs. of apricots soak in six qts. water for four days. Strain and add 6 lb. sugar to liquid. Cut, slice & peel 3 oranges & 2 lemons and add them to the liquid. Float a slice of toast on top of the liquid & sprinkle one package yeast on toast. After liquid has started to 'work' then remove the toast with yeast. After liquid stops 'working' strain it and put into a jar and let it stand for a month or longer. Strain again & bottle. Save for Christmas!

From a good friend in Barr'd Islands

RHUBARB BRANDY

6 lb. rhubarb	1 gallon water	1 lb. dates	4 lb. sugar
1 lb. barley	1 oz. yeast		

Wipe the rhubarb clean with a damp cloth, cut into mall pieces, and then crush with a rolling pin. Place the rhubarb in the water & allow to soak for 24 hours, crushing as much as possible during that time. Strain through muslin and put the juice through a jelly-bag. Bring the juice to boiling point and simmer for 3 minutes. Strain on to the sugar and stir until all the sugar is dissolved, then add the cut-up dates and the barley. Allow the brew to cool, sprinkle the yeast on top & stir in. Cover as directed & ferment for fourteen days, after which strain and proceed with the first bottling.

More good friends!

UNCLE ALLEN'S BLUEBERRY WINE

Wash 7 gallons of blueberries and put in Keg for two days. Then add 1 gallon molasses with enough water only to rinse out molasses can. Add 1 pound brown sugar, 1 yeast cake, 1 lb. raisins and 1 lb. prunes. Soak the raisins and prunes overnight before adding them along with the water they were soaked in. Cork the keg, but not too tight, and after three weeks, bottle it off.

"Nearest to port wine I've ever tasted. Real stuff!"

Mrs. Florence Wilkinson-Moores, Topsail

DOGBERRY WINE

Cook 2 qts. dogberries and 1 doz. apples (cut in pieces) in 4 qts. water. Strain. Add 8 cups sugar in a large crock. When lukewarm, add 1 package yeast. Store in a warm place until all bubbles have gone. Strain again and bottle.

HOW TO PRESERVE A HUSBAND

To Preserve a husband, be careful in your selection. Do not choose one too young, and take only such varieties as have been raised in a moral atmosphere. When once decided upon and selected, let that part remain forever settled and give your entire time and thought to domestic use.

Some insist on keeping them in pickle while others are constantly keeping them in hot water. Never keep them in ice. Even poor varieties may be made sweet and good by garnishing with patience, well seasoned with smiles and flavoured with kisses to taste.

Then wrap them up in a mantle of love, keep warm with a steady flow of devotion and serve with peaches and cream. When thus prepared they will keep for years.

Mrs. Allan Arbeau, St. Georges, Nfld.

KITCHEN KAPERS

FLOATING FAT: To remove floating fat from the surface of hot soup stock, use clean white blotting paper. *(Mrs. Hubert Freake, Fogo)*

DOUGHY HANDS. When making bread or pastry, always have two plastic bags near to put your hands in. If the phone rings or you have to answer the door, you're ready! *(Mrs. Bride Sheppard, Stag Harbour)*

PLAIN BISCUITS: If you find the plain biscuits from tins of assorted ones never seem to get eaten, sandwich them together in pairs with butter icing between them. Children love them. *(Mrs. Parmenas Wells)*

RED CABBAGE: Red cabbage will keep its colour if cooked with vinegar. Use 1 tsp. vinegar to 1 cup of water. Add when cabbage is partly cooked. *(Mrs. A. W. Freake)*

POTATO SALAD WITHOUT ONIONS: When you're making potato salad and don't like to eat onions but like the flavour of them, cut one large onion in fourths, place in the potato salad & let sit awhile. Before serving the salad, remove the onion. Some people also boil an onion in the water in which they are boiling the potatoes. The potatoes will absorb some of the flavour this way. *(Mrs. B.M. Penney)*

HARD SUGAR: Place a quarter of an apple in a tight container with sugar that has become hard. It will soften the hardest lump. *(Joan Brown)*

HOW TO BOIL A CRACKED EGG: If you have a little waxed paper about the house, try putting the egg in a twist of this and boil. You will be surprised to find that you have lost none of the contents. *(Cynthia Coish)*

REFRIGERATOR ODORS: Refrigerators should be cleaned regularly every season of the year, but particularly in the summer when they are used more frequently. If an odor persists after a thorough washing and rinsing, fill an empty coffee can with charcoal and set it inside on a middle shelf. Sometimes a slice or two of white bread helps too.

EGG STAINS: To remove egg stains from spoons & forks, take a little salt between thumb & forefinger & rub briskly.
(Cynthia Coish,Stag Harbour)

SHARPEN SCISSORS: Scissors may be sharpened by cutting through fine sandpaper several times.
(Mrs.Margaret Freake, Joe Batt's Arm)

YELLOW LINENS: Yellow linens may become white by putting a few drops of turpentine in the rinse water, and then hang in the sun to bleach.
Margaret Freake, Joe Batt's Arm.

PLASTERED WALLS: To keep plastered walls from cracking when driving a picture hook into the wall, first cut a piece of adhesive tape and stick it to the wall. Then drive the nail into taped wall.
(Alma Payne - Fogo)

PAINTING CUPBOARDS: To avoid smearing window glass or cupboard door pulls when painting, grease the glass and pulls with vasoline. This prevents paint from sticking. When paint drys, wipe off vasoline.
(Mrs. Joyce Anthony, Seldom)

HOUSE PLANTS: Brighten your house plants with a milk bath. Take a small cloth and a saucer of milk and sponge the leaves with a thin coating of milk. Makes the leaves shine and removes dust.
(Mrs. Maude Freake - Joe Batt's Arm)

SWEATER CUFFS: When knitting children's sweaters, start the sleeves at the armhole and work them down to the cuff. As the child grows, it is easier to knit a piece to the end of the cuff.
(Mrs. Wesley Sheppard, Stag Harbour)

UNTASTY MEDICINE: Before children have to take a dose of unpleasant tasting medicine, give them an ice cube to suck. This will make the taste of the medicine less noticeable.
(Mrs. Hubert Freake, Fogo)

I HAVE NOT TIME TO BE A SAINT
Lord of all pots and pans and things,
Since I have not time to be
A saint by doing lovely things -
Or watching late with thee,
Or dreaming in the dawn light,
Or storming heaven's gates;
Make me a saint by getting meals
And washing up the plates.
Warm all the kitchen with thy love
And light it with thy peace;
Forgive me all my worrying
And make my grumbling cease.
Thou who did' st love to give men food,
 In room or by the sea,
Accept the service that I do -
I do it unto Thee.
Submitted by Nora Leyte - Fogo

ALL SET FOR THE NIGHT
The hostess of a hospitality home in Fogo looked at her two guests who appeared collectively oversized for the bed in the guest room.

"Here," she said to the husband, whose wife was the larger of the two, "I'll put yer longliner t' rest in the guest room, an' ye, y' little dory, ye'll hav' t' sleep alone on the couch down th' 'all."

SUNSHINE CAKE
Fill a measure full of sunshine,
Some crumbs of comfort too;
Then mix them well with loving thoughts
And words both kind and true.
Let them quickly rise with action
To deeds of golden hue,
And you'll have a cake worth eating
When baking time is through.
Yes, you'll have a life worth living
And a cure for every ache
If you and all your family
Will feast on Sunshine Cake.
Gladys Garland, Lower Island Cove

A GOOD COOK
She guessed at the pepper, the soup was too hot.
She guessed at the water, it dried in the pot.
She guessed at the salt and what do you think?
For the rest of the day, we did nothing but drink:
She guessed at the sugar, the sauce was too sweet,
And by guessing, she spoiled the meat.
What is the moral? It's easy to see -
A good cook measures and weighs to a 'T'.
Submitted by Stella Decker - Joe Batt's Arm

TAKE TIME FOR TEN THINGS

Take time to **work**, for it is the price of success.
Take time to **think**, for it is the source of power.
Take time to **play**, for it is the secret of youth.
Take time to **read**, for it is the foundation of knowledge.
Take time for **worship**, for it is the highway of reverence and washes the dust of earth from your eyes.
Take time to **help** and **enjoy friends**, for this is the source of happiness.
Take time to **love**, for it is the one sacrament of life.
Take time to **dream**, for it hitches the soul to the stars.
Take time to **laugh**, for it is the singing that helps with life's loads.
Take time to **plan**, for it is the secret of being able to have time for the first nine things.

Submitted by Mrs. Stella Collins - Stag Harbour

"He smoked like a winter tilt." - A tilt was the temporary shelter built in the woods and occupied only when men go inland to cut wood or hunt. *Submitted by Mrs. Roy Anthony - Seldom*

"You can't tell the mind of a squid." - This refers to an unreliable person. A squid moves backward or forward at a moment's notice. *Submitted by Mrs. William H. Anthony - Seldom*

"Some animals would be as smart as men, if they could talk."

A bit of local wisdom submitted by Mrs. Melvin Holmes - Seldom

The shortest conversation held between two fishermen: "Ar'n?" "Nar'n."
'Ar'n' meaning, 'Did you get any fish. 'Nar' n' meaning,'No, none.'

Another fisherman's conversation: "How's the fish this year?" Reply: "Not so good. Them that ar'n ain't no better than them that nar'n; cause them that got nar'n, ain't no bit of size."

Submitted by Mrs. Roy Anthony - Seldom Come By

THE PARTING

I've spent so many hours with you,
  And planned so many things to do;
While bending over you, it seems
  You're part and parcel of all my dreams.
I've stood by you down through the years,
  Sometimes with smiles, sometimes with tears;
And countless are the little prayers
  I've breathed upon you unawares.
But you have changed - and oh, how much,
  You shiver at my slightest touch
And walk away from me indeed
  When pressing is my want or need.
Old Ironing Board, your day is done —
  I'll have to get anohter one!

Mrs. Florence Wilkinson-Moores, Topsail

FOGO ISLAND EXPRESSIONS

Hold on to your wool! -   Slow down!
Good as the weather -   Feeling well.
Half and a quarter well. -   Feeling okay.
Going out to squeeze me brewis. -
    Going outside to use the bathroom.
**There's better fish in the water than have been
pulled out.** - Don't worry about the boyfriend
you've lost because there are better ones to get.

Peggy Jones & Beth Walbourne - Fogo

FOGO

Fogo has nice houses,
It has nice people too.
They are all friendly
With me and with you.
There's not much pollution here,
The air is very clean;
I think this is the nicest place
I have ever seen!

Inez Torraville - Fogo

SEALING

When the ice comes in the bay,
"The seals will soon be here,"
    the men all say.
The ice will soon be packed in tight
And the men try to kill seals
    with all their might.
The men grease their guns
And pack a lunch of tea and buns.
They leave home in early morning
And kill the seals without warning.

By Elaine Day - Grade 8 - Seldom

RECIPE FOR OLD TIME BARM (Yeast)

hops   potatoes   boiling water   molasses

The principal ingredient for Barm was hops. As long as I can remember, hops could be bought in small packages in stores. My mother used to grow her own supply of hops. She dried them for winter use and shared some with her neighbours.

The hops would be boiled, strained through thin material and the water put in a bottle. Potatoes would be grated fine and added to the bottle with a portion of molasses. A cork would be inserted in the bottle and a string tied around the neck. The bottle and contents would then be hung on a nail in the wall behind the Waterloo or Comfort stove.

For the next couple days the bottle would be shaken at intervals. It would then be ready to raise bread. Bread raised today with modern yeast cannot compare in taste or texture to the bread of yesteryears, especially if baked in an iron bake pot.   *Victor Butler (80 years of age), Arnold's Cove, P.B., Nfld.*

MRS. IDA DICKS SPECIAL SPRUCE BEER RECIPE

First, she would proceed to the woods and was very particular in selecting the tops of small dark green black spruce trees. The tops would be boiled and strained through material and the liquid placed in a large earthern-ware jar or a small oak keg.

Molasses would be added. Some barm, mentioned above, would be added. Raisins, if available, would also be added to the liquid. A secure cork would be placed in the utensil. The jar and contents would then be placed in a warm place to brew.

For years passed, when peanut butter was available in stores for sale, the butter would be contained in twenty-five pound buckets. It would then be sold in small amounts as required by the customer. Peanut butter was a luxury at the time I am referring to. Mrs. Dicks and her daughters were fond of peanut butter. I heard her say, "With a couple of peanut butter sandwiches and a portion of spruce beer," they were ready to proceed to the barrens to pick partirdgeberries.

Victor Butler, Arnold's Cove, P.B., Nfld.

"I HOPE YOU SELL MILLIONS OF COPIES"

Point Claire, Que.
March 8, 1975

Dear Reverend:

I received a copy of "Fat-Back & Molasses" as a gift from a friend when we lived in Nfld. last year, and a relative of mine saw it and asked if there was any possibility of her getting one.

Incidentally, the recipes contained in the book are the most dependable ones I have tried yet. No hesitation on trying any of them, after having lived in Nfld. for a while — delicious recipes and not expensive.

K. Mankinen

Whidden Memorial Hospital
Everett, Massachusetts
May 29, 1975

Dear Rev. Jesperson,

One of our employees brought in a cook book with all of the most wonderful recipes from Newfoundland and Labrador. I found it most intriguing and interesting. I was wondering if you would be so kind as to find out if I can purchase a dozen of these books. I would like several and some of our employees would like one too.

Sincerely yours,
Mildred B. Malcolm

Willowdale, Ontario
September 8, 1975

Dear Rev. Jesperson,

I would like to thank you for the prompt delivery of my two copies of "Fat Back & Molasses". I am taking home a copy to my mother in Newfoundland in October and I'm sure she will appreciate it as much as I do. I hope you will sell millions of copies of this fantastic book.

Thanking you again,
Yours faithfully,
Vonne Simmonds

Swan River, Manitoba
July 25, 1975

Dear Sirs,

Through a friend, a collector of cook books as myself, I borrowed "Fat Back & Molasses".

How could I have missed such an excellent cook book and pure Canadian. This book has also many dishes as used in the country in which I was born. I would like to know as to where I could obtain hard-tack. Surely this is a produce unknown in the West. However, my mother used this so often in cooking.

Yours truly,
W.S. Howes

Germany
February 14, 1977

Dear Rev. Jesperson

First of all I'll explain why I'm writing to you. This eveing my husband came from work with a copy of the Nfld. cookbook "Fat Back & Molasses" and since I'm a former Newfoundlander I really was delighted to read it. However, the book has to be returned but I certainly would like one for myself. I especially enjoyed the writing about Harvest Supper, Bon Fire and Mummers.

My husband, myself and daughter are doing a four year posting here in Germany. So far we have almost 3 years spent here which leaves only one left here. We are enjoying ourselves very much. We live in a little German town and the German people are really nice to us.

Please wriite if you can still supply me with a cook book and let me kdnow the cost so I can get some money changed into Canadian currency.

We lived six and one-half years in good old St. John's before our posting here.

Thank you and best wishes,
Mrs. Winifred J. McCullough

Waterloo, Iowa,
U.S.A.
November 4, 1975

Dear Pastor Jesperson:

My husband and I have jsut returned from a trip to the New England States where we visited members of my family. All of us having been born in Nfld. have a real yen for the homey things of the Island. One of my Aunts had spent some time there last year and during the course of our conversation she mentioned a cook book purchased at that time. The title itself intrigued me, and after a quick glance through some of the contents, I knew I must have one.

If copies are still available, please advise me as to the cost and postage, and I will send you a cheque by return mail. Some of the recipes would be ideal for use at Christmas time when home made goodies are so welcomed by our "shut-ins."

Yours truly,
Judy Brechenfelder

Any Mummers in the night?

OUR FIRST CHRISTMAS IN NEWFOUNDLAND — The door bell rang. Visitors, we thought, to help us celebrate the joys of the season. We opened the door."Any mummers in the night?" The voice crackled with squeeks and half-tones from behind a flour-sack hood. "Any mummers in the night?" another voice drew in. Obviously the visitors were as surprised by our lack of understanding as we were by their manner of dress. The visitors, we later learned, were 'Mummers' who went from house to house between Christmas and January 6th (referred to as 'Old Christmas Day') to entertain their surprised hosts, enjoy themselves and visit friends and foe alike. The costumes and masks help keep identity a secret and adds to the merriment of a beautiful Newfoundland tradition.